Portraits of Teachers in Multicultural Settings

A Critical Literacy Approach

Lettie Ramírez
Olivia M. Gallardo
California State University, Hayward

Allyn and Bacon
Boston • London • Toronto • Sydney • Tokyo • Singapore

Series editor: Traci Mueller
Series editorial assistant: Bridget Keane
Marketing manager: Brad Parkins

Library of Congress Cataloging-in-Publication Data

Portraits of teachers in multicultural settings : a critical literacy approach / [edited by]
Lettie Ramírez, Olivia M. Gallardo.
    p. cm.
  Includes bibliographical references and index.
  ISBN 0-205-30575-X
    1. Critical pedagogy--United States. 2. Multicultural education--United States. 3.
Language arts--United States. 4. Education--Parent participation--United States. I.
Ramírez, Lettie. II. Gallardo, Olivia M.
  LC196.5.U6 P67 2001
  370.117--dc21   00-063948

Printed in the United States of America
10   9   8   7   6   5   4   3   2   1   05   04   03   02   01

Contents

PART I   Introduction

PART II   *Empowerment: Beyond the Deficits and into Reading and Writing*

PART III   *Enhancing the Curriculum Using Critical Fine Art Literacy*

PART IV   *The Future of Classroom Technology: Critical Responses*

Foreword

To educate a nation's youth has been a determination of every human culture. Although the commitment to pass on knowledge and skills and to foster abilities has been constant, the ultimate purpose of education has been diverse. It may be seen as inserted between two polar goals. On one side is the self-serving need of the adults to train youth to serve the older generations—whether by obtaining or securing more territory, by providing food, or by constructing shelter or improving the living standards of the group. On the other side is the selfless desire of giving the youth an opportunity to develop as fully as possible for their own sake.

This dichotomous description, as with all dichotomies, suffers from oversimplification. It is possible that the ultimate goals of the adults who set out to educate youth may contain multiple elements. The preservation of a culture and a worldview and the fulfillment of ideals may have become somewhat intertwined with the material needs fulfilled by youth.

The reality is that, in most instances, education has not been equally provided to all youth, nor with the same objectives. In most societies, some youth have been educated to provide for others, and some have been predetermined to realize menial tasks in order that others may enjoy the fulfillment of the intellect or the spirit.

When the concept of democracy is incorporated into the educational foundation of a society, it becomes critical to analyze to what extent the educational system promotes the development of a just, equitable society with similar opportunities for all, or whether the democratic label is being used to hide an educational system developed for the maintenance of existing societal privileges. While taking on the self-defined role of the defender of democracy in the world, the United States has allowed its society to become more divergent with regard to basic human needs. With a small number becoming richer and a very large number—mainly of people of color, and in particular women and children—becoming poorer, we are forced to question the role of education in the perpetuation of what Jonathan Kozol has labeled "savage inequalities."

Educators committed to promoting an education that recognizes the human potential of each individual and fosters his or her development, regardless of the social conditions surrounding the person's birth and upbringing, need to search for educational principles that support a liberatory praxis. These principles can be found within an encompassing umbrella loosely defined as *transformative education*. This is not a method or a technique with specific steps, but rather a synthesis of theoretical principles with a very clear social stand on issues concerning equity, inclusion, justice, and peace. Probably when asked to describe it, each transformative education theorist would ascribe different values to the various components.

Transformative education derives from critical theory as exposed by the philosophers of the School of Frankfurt and brought to education with great clarity by Paulo Freire. Critical theory expresses that human beings are the sole constructors of social reality and, as such, are responsible for participating in its ongoing creation, as well as in its improvement, through the search for justice.

On developing critical pedagogy based on these theories, Freire points out, without hesitation, that throughout the world most forms of public or massive education promote the domestication and colonization of the human mind in order to maintain the status quo. He also suggests that the hope for justice is directly dependent on the building of awareness in those who are the victims of the system—that they will join in solidarity and build the necessary strength to search for their emancipation and that of all others, since unjust conditions are dehumanizing to all.

If I were to define transformative education as I practice it, I would see it primarily as a determination to foster the human essence. As such, it complements critical pedagogy by embracing the constructivist principle that all human beings are beings of knowledge, engaged in the continuous process of making sense of their world and having an intrinsic desire to learn and an innate ability to grow and develop. And because human beings are essentially beings of love and care, transformative education also embraces the womanist theories, which support learning in a safe, nurturing environment.

Recognizing that human beings are intrinsically drawn to beauty, as evidenced by the examples from cultures all over the world, which have consistently aimed at creating beauty, transformative education needs to pay attention to the aesthetic aspects of growth. It must also recognize multiculturalism as the basis of human interaction. The earth is diverse by its very nature. Human beings are as diverse as the reality of this planet. Dominant cultures create an image of the "norm" to exclude those not fitting a narrowly defined category, but in reality, the only norm of human existence is its own diversity.

This diversity is expressed also through the multiple languages human beings have created. Because language is one of the strongest elements in our self-definition, as well as one of the key elements of a culture, true transformative education must embrace bilingual education for all. It will serve as a way of retention and development of every child's mother tongue and as the opportunity for all to achieve the understanding for other cultures that can only be fully attained once every person has learned at least one other language besides his or her own.

Finally, because prejudice and biases have been prevalent throughout human history, and because most cultures are ethnocentric, transformative education must become anti-bias education, denouncing the dangers of racism, which create injustice and can generate a climate leading to destructive behavior against other human beings. To become fully human, we must unlearn prejudice and bias and become each other's allies.

These principles are often difficult to express because they become a denunciation of things we wish did not exist. They are far more difficult to implement, for they demand unlearning much of what has been inculcated on us, going against usual trends, making others feel uncomfortable with their complacence, and above all because they demand constant reflection and self-examination. Furthermore, educators who are willing to initiate a process of self-transformation, as well as a transformation of their educational environment, find the road uncharted.

As Antonio Machado has said, and Paulo Freire has embraced in the title of one of his books, *We Make the Road by Walking,* the examples of others can become invaluable companions in the opening of new roads. The gift of this book is twofold: the depth of the reflection of the authors of the chapters, and their willingness to share their practices.

It is an honor to have known most of them along the same road of hope. May you find their words as inspiring as I find their lives.

Alma Flor Ada

Preface

Portraits of Teachers in Multicultural Settings highlights the work of leading practitioners in the field of transformative education. This book is based on the assumptions that multicultural education goes far beyond the holidays, celebrations, and heroes that classroom teachers highlight at special times of the year. Multicultural education is an extension of one's lived experiences, and as such, the recognition of the profound value of the human being cannot be minimized to only certain months of the year.

The populations of schools continuously change. However, not all schools reflect the cultures that are representative of U.S. society. In this book, practicing educators who have lived and worked in various parts of the world and the United States share their experiences and describe the processes they use to make their classrooms inclusive of the mosaic of cultures represented in their classrooms. The use of critical theory as a foundation for the incorporation of multicultural education results in students learning about themselves and the world around them. Each chapter describes the awakening the authors discovered in themselves and in their students as the interaction and dialogues focused on their students' lived experiences.

The chapters are divided into various sections highlighting the practitioners' work in and out of the classroom. Educators in their particular fields define the role of critical literacy in the empowerment process and how it actuates itself within their disciplines. The first chapter introduces and defines critical literacy and the application of its principles. The next three chapters highlight the use of critical literacy in the classroom, discuss the appropriate selection of books, and describe the process the teachers found to work best for their students. Chapters 5 and 6 describe the use of critical art literacy. The social constructs of a particular time or place and its effects on social relations are examined through art, history, and drama. Students begin to formulate thoughts and questions on how and why knowledge gets constructed the way it does and how it benefits some and not others. Chapters 7 and 8 examine the technology that transforms writing. The creative writing process, highlighted in Chapter 7, describes how a student moves from the initial phase of communication to the creative phase. Chapter 8 continues by explaining the multicultural implications in the use of technology and how it adds to the transformative process in each individual.

Chapters 9 and 10 address the needs of school/parent/child relationships. The sociocultural needs of the individual are discussed within the framework of a school setting, focusing on children of color. Chapters 11 and 12 examine the issues that affect educators as the cultural setting in the classroom begins to change. The Epilogue summarizes various viewpoints of authors who speak to the need for change and reminds the reader that to be committed to transformative education, one must be willing to be transformed. It means dealing with the "-isms" of life.

Together, as one voice, the authors of these chapters search for methodologies that promote a love for humanity and each other, a respect for the individual's cultural and linguistic differences, and an equitable environment promoting learning experiences that lead to personal and career growth. The vision of these practitioners is to move beyond knowing to making a change.

Acknowledgments

This book would not have been possible without the dedication and expertise of the contributing authors. They opened their hearts and shared with us their classroom practices.

We thank Dr. Alma Flor Ada and the Title VII Fellows and Colleagues from the University of San Francisco. Their support and encouragement has been ongoing. The special words of Duarte Silva, Peter Baird, and Guadalupe Solis helped us greatly.

Others whose comments and suggestions were vital to this book include colleagues from the University of Texas Pan American; Mary Valerio, California State University, Hayward; Linda Lambert and Joan Davenport, University of Pennsylvania; and reviewers Debbie Harmon, Colorado State University; Dale Titus, Kutztown University of Pennsylvania; and Russell Young, San Diego State University.

Thank you, also, to our current and former students for continuing to pursue transformative principles that lead toward equity and justice. A special thank you to Diana Encarnacion, whose fervor and spirit have helped many students find Freire's words and apply his principle.

Finally, all of this would not have been possible without the help from Allyn and Bacon's series editor Traci Mueller, series editorial assistant Bridget Keane, and marketing manager Brad Parkins, and from Lynda Griffiths at TKM Productions.

Lettie Ramírez
Olivia M. Gallardo

About the Authors

Lettie Ramírez is an associate professor at California State University, Hayward. She is director of Project SABER, a career ladder program that supports high school students and instructional assistants to become bilingual teachers. She also coordinates the Bilingual and Special Education Teacher Education Program. Ramírez works with various school districts and county offices as a consultant on multicultural education programs. Active in the bilingual multicultural movement since 1982, she has conducted numerous presentations in state, national, and international conferences. Ramírez received her doctorate from the University of Texas in Austin and worked with the Southwest Educational Development Laboratory in Austin prior to coming to California.

Olivia M. Gallardo is a lecturer and student teacher supervisor at California State University, Hayward, and Saint Mary's College. She has a master's degree in urban education with an emphasis in bilingual models as well as an administrative and reading resource credential. Gallardo has 20 years of teaching experience in bilingual classrooms at the middle and elementary school levels and as an English language development specialist at the high school level. Her interests focus on issues of language and cultural equity for parents and children. Gallardo received her doctorate in international multicultural education from the University of San Francisco.

About the Contributors

Valerie Andriola Balderas is a former Title VII Doctoral Fellow from the University of San Francisco. She is an artist/teacher whose work has taken her into various communities of the Southwest. Currently she works in New Mexico with secondary students. Her publications include *To Be Alive in Struggle: One Teacher's Journey in Reclaiming Our Voices* (1995) from the California Association of Bilingual Educators, in Ontario, California.

Rosario Díaz-Greenberg is an associate professor of bilingual/bicultural studies at California State University, San Marcos. She has worked in various parts of the country, including New York City schools and Dade County Public Schools in Miami, Florida, as a teacher of native language arts. She has also taught in a state department-sponsored school in her native country of El Salvador. Díaz-Greenberg is a former Title VII fellowship recipient, and has completed her studies at the University of San Francisco in international/multicultural education.

Bijan B. Gillani is an associate professor and the director of the graduate program in educational technology leadership at California State University, Hayward. He received his doctorate in curriculum and technology from the University of Southern California. Gillani specializes in the application of developmental theories in the design of educational multimedia and the Web. He teaches graduate courses in learning theories and multimedia design, educational interface design, current technologies, and educational psychology. He has published articles and has presented at conferences on the topic of the integration of multimedia and the Web in education. Currently, Gillani is completing a book on Web design.

R. Greg Jennings is an associate professor at California State University, Hayward, in educational psychology. He received his doctorate from University of California, Berkeley, in educational psychology and his master's from University of California, Santa Barbara, in counseling psychology. A school psychologist by training, Jennings has trained graduate students at California State University, Hayward, as future school psychologists. His research interests are children's resiliency, their capacity to bounce back in spite of adversity, their emotional understanding, their thinking about how emotions work, and classroom factors that influence their learning. Jennings continues to be a practicing school psychologist in northern California. His experiences in working with families have inspired him to begin developing resiliency fostering inservices for schools. He advocates a respect for children's individual resiliency strengths and speaks out against the media's preoccupation with "at-risk" labels for minority and poor children.

Margaret C. Laughlin is an associate professor of literacy/biliteracy at the Center for Collaborative Education and Professional Studies at California State University, Monterey Bay. She is a former Title VII fellow recipient. She received her doctorate in international and multicultural education from the University of San Francisco. Laughlin's vision is to see the growth of support in the field of critical multicultural education. She appreciates that it takes a lot of courage to teach for inclusion, and in ways that value all students as human beings.

José A. López is an associate professor at California State University, Hayward, in the Department of Educational Leadership. His major responsibility is working with teacher leaders in the educational leader preparation program leading to the California administrative credential. Prior to university teaching, López served in various administrative capacities in Texas school districts. These positions included principal, area superintendent, and superintendent.

Julia Marshall is an assistant professor at San Francisco State University, where she teaches courses in learning and instruction in visual art. She received her Ed.D. in multicultural education from the University of San Francisco and is a professional artist and consultant on curriculum development to educational and exhibiting institutions in the Bay Area.

Aspasia Neophytos-Richardson is an assistant professor at Chapman University. She received her doctorate from the University of San Francisco, and her current research focuses on western history from a gender-equity perspective. An educator, interculturalist, writer, and artist, she speaks Greek, Afrikaans, Spanish, and French and has lived, worked, and studied on five continents.

Mary-Louise Newling is an adjunct professor in the school of education at the University of San Francisco. In addition, she teaches fifth grade and incorporates multicultural curriculum in her classroom. She also serves as a teacher consultant with the Bay Area Writing Project. Newling has taught both in her native Trinidad and Tobago and in the United States. Her dissertation topic was "Reflections of Rebel Women of the African Diaspora." She obtained her Ed.D. from the University of San Francisco.

Folásadé Oládélé was born in Louisville, Kentucky, and educated in the Louisville public schools. She received a B.S. degree in music and English from Indiana University, Bloomington, and a master's degree in education from Holy Names College, Oakland, California. She is currently the program manager of language, literacy, and African American culture for the Oakland Unified School District. In addition, Oládélé is currently an adjunct professor at the University of San Francisco, where she obtained her doctorate studies in international and multicultural education. Her publications include "Giving Voice to the Voiceless," *Harvard Educational Review* (Spring 1993); "Spirit: The Heart of Education," *Educational Leadership* (December 1998); and *Awakening Students' Talents: A Teacher's Guide to Developing Skills in Reading, Thinking and Writing* (1998), Meroe Publishing Company in Berkeley, California.

Jacquelyn Valerie Reza is currently a professor at De Anza College and a practicing licensed Marriage, Family, and Child Therapist (MFCT). She teaches in the Women's Studies and Intercultural

Studies Departments. Reza received her doctorate in international and multicultural education from the University of San Francisco and obtained her B.S. degree in zoology, with an emphasis in ornithology, from Ahmadu Bello University in Nigeria, West Africa. She received her second bachelor's degree in La Raza Studies, and an M.S. in rehabilitation counseling. She is a former Title VII fellowship recipient. In addition to her work at De Anza College, Reza has been an oral examiner for the California Board of Behavioral Science Examiners for the Marriage, Family, and Child counselor licensing examinations. She also maintains a private consulting business and gives workshops and seminars around the country on interpersonal dynamics that focus on multicultural and women's issues.

Nancy Jean Smith is a former Title VII Doctoral Fellow from the University of San Francisco. Much of her research and writing have focused on authentic and critical literacy, language loss and linguistic genocide, and participatory research and inclusive multicultural pedagogies created through transformative education. Currently she is an associate professor in the Teacher Education Department at the California State University, Stanislaus MCRC Stockton Campus.

1

Beyond Multicultural Education
Transformative Approaches

LETTIE RAMÍREZ   *OLIVIA M. GALLARDO*

Portraits of Teachers in Multicultural Settings evolved as a result of our work with teachers and future teachers. An understanding of what *multicultural education* meant was often confused with holidays, activities, and literature books that depict people of various ethnic groups, mainly people of color (Lee, Menkart, & Okazawa-Rey, 1998). The activities and books we found many times lacked any correlation to theory or research. Teachers were using certain material on designated holidays instead of integrating cross-cultural education into their curriculum. One book in particular that we found breaking through the celebrations themes, *Beyond Heroes and Holidays* (Lee, Menkart, & Okazawa-Rey, 1998), provides readers with a practical guide that brings together strategies and examples of teachers' work based on the philosophy of critical pedagogy. Educators new to the field of multicultural education often ask for examples on how to integrate multicultural education into the everyday curriculum year round. The contributing authors in this book felt that a major need existed to demonstrate what a classroom looks like that integrates culture and language into its daily routine, forming part of the challenging curriculum teachers need to follow. With this in mind, the portraits of educators who incorporate a critical literacy approach in their teaching present a variety of experiences in how teaching leads to exciting lessons that motivate students to learn. We trust that teachers can adapt, modify, and create new programs that fit their teaching styles once they are given a foundation on what we call *transformative teaching* based on critical theory.

Educators throughout the world are finding that transformative principles instill in the learner a new excitement for learning. Celestin Freinet, referred to as the Dewey of Europe (Temple & Rodero, 1995), established a school in France known as the *École Moderne* (or Modern School) in 1950. His innovative work has withstood the test of time and has been translated into Arabic, Danish, Dutch, German, Greek, Hungarian, Italian, Japanese, Norwegian, Polish, Portuguese, Russian, Spanish, Swedish, Vietnamese, and even into Catalan, Basque, and Esperanto, yet little is known of Freinet in the United States. His words justify what we believe is the key to transformative teaching: "Un método, si es bueno, debe ser válido en todas las clases y en todas partes [A method, if it is a good one, should be valid with all classes and in all places]" (Freinet, 1994, p. 40).

Transformative education as a movement has a long history and is seen as an outgrowth of critical pedagogy pioneered by Brazilian educator, Paulo Freire. It combines its principles with those of constructivism and feminist theory. Ada and Campoy (2000) further clarify:

> *The process of transformative pedagogy relies on constructivist principles, the creation of loving and caring relationships and environments, and the strengths of the arts. It recognizes diversity as essential to life, and fosters respect for all forms of diversity. . . . All of the various aspects of intelligence are addressed and critical and reflective abilities are strengthened through practices that are interactive, creative and joyful. Finally, transformative pedagogy recognizes the prevalence of biases and prejudice, and acknowledges the need to*

unlearn racist practices and assumptions as an essential
ingredient for the creation of a just society. (p. 39)

Critical educators recognize that they cannot change a student's circumstances or environments; however, they find that they can act as agents of change through critically examining how traditional education promotes or hinders the student's success or failure. Teacher and student alike work together to become part of the problem-solving process. This teaching goes beyond the celebration of ethnic holidays and into the heart of what is known as a "humanizing pedagogy." Cummins (1996) expands the notion of this process by adding that identity and empowerment come from human relationships. The purposes, anxieties, and relationships of the individuals served cannot be ignored. The teacher/student relationship is at the heart of schooling.

A critical theory of teaching and learning as Darder (1991) explains was born out of inquiry and concern, with its emphasis on the understanding that it is only through an examination of the link between culture and power that a cultural democracy can emerge. McLaren (1998) offers these inquiries on critical pedagogy and its relation to cultural democracy: "Critical pedagogy asks how and why knowledge gets constructed the way it does and why some constructions of reality are legitimated and celebrated by the dominant culture while others clearly are not" (p. 174). Transformative education encourages teachers and students to begin focusing simultaneously on both sides of a social contradiction and working toward ending these contradictions.

Each chapter in this book will provide answers to these questions. The text will look at multicultural education and provide classroom experiences that promote opening dialogue between teacher and student, leading to reflection and action. Transformative education models work with all students. Freire and Macedo (1987) believe that the educator enters into a world where reading the world takes precedence to reading the word (p. 35). This world refers to all children. Teacher and students together find voice to their own stories and experiences. Knowledge becomes a means for examining what they know, and either they affirm and accept or continue reworking their assumptions. Lifeless discourse is replaced by active, expressive voices. Apathy and rote learning are replaced by problem-posing students seeking solutions. Cummins (1996) refers to this evolution as developing a sense of self. He feels that students' positive affirmations will extend to others and that they are more likely to apply themselves to academic effort and participate actively in instruction. The consequent learning is the fuel generating further academic effort. The more one learns, the more one wants to learn (p. 2).

Literacy at this juncture becomes critical. The transformation of education from a project of social control to one of self and social empowerment is at the heart of all forms of pedagogy that claim the adjective *critical* (Frederickson, 1998). The key components effectively move students and teachers toward changes in attitude and performance. This "empowerment" process leads to independent knowledge that extends beyond the classroom. Multicultural teaching is not an event but an everyday tool used to break down the structures and practices that either oppress or privilege people on the basis of socially constructed categories that have commonly become known as *–isms*. The rationale is that instruction must evoke intellectual effort on the part of the students. If the instruction is cognitively undemanding, students will learn very little and quickly become bored in the process (Cummins, 1996).

To bridge the gap between a student's culture and the culture of the school, the following principles comprise the transformative ideals of this book:

1. Classroom curriculum is connected to real-life experiences.
2. Through critical literature, the past and the present are embraced.
3. Students and their cultures are valued and respected.
4. Shared decision making in a democratic community is practiced.
5. Meaningful parent involvement is practiced.
6. In a solution-seeking curriculum, risk taking is encouraged in safe environments for all students.
7. Curriculum and lessons promote equity and social justice.

Multicultural education transcends color. Its curriculum recognizes the profound value of all human beings and the richness that diversity brings to any nation, and certainly to the world. Multicultural education also transcends disciplines. Educators working with children from many areas and in varied conditions present lessons attending to the needs of the children.

Within the current educational system, students are labeled and often prematurely categorized as "disadvantaged," "disenfranchised," and "at risk." The possibilities within a transformative framework speak about hope, inclusion, and equity—all within the capabilities of a teacher, school, and district. The vision of the practitioners in the field of multicultural education is to move beyond knowing that change is needed to actually making that change. Herein lies the essence of what transformative education means. Teachers seeking answers to the inequities existing in the classroom for whatever the reasons find solutions by beginning with a change in the exclusionary practices.

Fusing Multicultural Education and Critical Theory

In the United States, educators live and work in multicultural societies of students who vary by ethnicity, language background, and socioeconomic status. The educators must choose what and how to teach in classrooms while honoring both diversity and excellence. Nieto (1992) writes,

> *Teachers genuinely do not want to believe that some children are inferior to others or that the culture of their students is what causes their school failure.... Yet it is not unusual for teachers, after having worked with a great many youths, to start accepting the belief that children from some ethnicities or racial groups may indeed be inherently "better" students than others. Nothing seems to work, and the same young people are dropping out and failing. (p. 1)*

Although most approaches to multicultural education have paid lip service to the notion that cultural diversity contributes positively to society, not surprisingly, they did not look critically at dominant group power and its role in the oppression of certain cultural groups through either assimilation or an acculturation model. Those groups joining the majority lacked the multicultural resources to help others of their cultural and ethnic groups succeed. The nation's history is replete with examples.

Research in the area of multicultural education has been influenced by the seminal work of James Banks (1994, 1997). He brought to light the inconsistency with which textbooks incorporate in-depth knowledge about ethnic cultures and experiences into the curriculum and how mainstream-centric curriculum supports, reinforces, and justifies the existing social, economic, and political structure. Banks helped transform multicultural education with his formulation of Approaches to Multicultural Curriculum Reform. These approaches are organized into a framework that guides teachers of diverse population and are further addressed in Chapters 2 and 7.

At the lower level, the Contributions Approach, classroom activities focus on heroes, holidays, and discrete cultural elements. At the second level, the Additive Approach, content, concepts, themes, and perspectives are added to the curriculum without changing its structure. Level three, the Transformation Approach, changes the structure of the curriculum to enable students to view concepts, issues, events, and themes from the perspective of diverse ethnic and cultural groups. At the fourth level, the Social Action Approach, students make decisions on social issues important to their lives and take action to help solve them. At this level, the missing element of students' participation in their learning is finally addressed. With this approach, Banks gave multicultural education the solid pedagogic framework that teachers recognized as essential to place students at the center of their self-discovery and as contributing agents for positive change in their schools and communities. This approach prepares teachers and students to change society, to better serve all people. It is at this exact intersection that critical teaching and multicultural education connect, with a common goal of creating a school environment that engenders pluralism through active involvement and equal educational opportunities where differences and similarities are valued and respected. Empowerment teaching is characterized by a strong whole-school community that validates students' language and culture, promotes parent and community participation, and participates in critical and independent learning (Cummins, 1995).

To guide multicultural teachers, Walsh (1991) synthesizes the basic tenets of critical teaching and learning as follows:

1. Education is not neutral.
2. Learners learn not by acquiring facts but by constructing knowledge in social exchange with others.
3. There are social, cultural, and ideological conditions that shape the construction of knowledge and the development of meaning at home, in the community, and at school. The structural forces at work in society influence these conditions.
4. The role of teacher is one of co-learner, listener, and facilitator, not owner or conveyor of knowledge.
5. Education should enable students to develop heightened awareness about and take enlightened action toward the creation of a just society. In this sense, education signifies interventions.

Transformative education utilizing multicultural education frameworks can move students and teachers beyond empowerment. The common goal moves all students toward the control of their own lives, communicating and sharing together beyond cultural and racial boundaries. Educators are encouraged to examine their own teaching as they begin their journey with *Portraits of Teachers in Multicultural Settings*.

References

Ada, A. F., & Campoy, F. I. (2000). *Readings on anti-bias education curriculum: A theoretical introduction*. San Francisco: University of San Francisco.

Banks, J. (1994). *An introduction to multicultural education*. Boston: Allyn and Bacon.

Banks, J. (1997). Multicultural education. In J. Banks & C. Banks (Eds.), *Multicultural education: Issues and perspectives* (3rd ed.). Boston: Allyn and Bacon.

Cummins, J. (1995). Knowledge, power, and identity in teaching English as a second language. In F. Genesee (Ed.), *Educating second language children: The whole child, the whole curriculum, the whole community* (3rd ed.). Cambridge: Cambridge University Press.

Cummins, J. (1996). *Negotiating identities: Education for empowerment in a diverse society.* Ontario, CA: California Association for Bilingual Educators.

Darder, A. (1991). *Culture and power in the classroom.* New York: Bergin & Garvey.

Frederickson, J. (1998). *Reclaiming our voices.* Ontario, CA: California Association for Bilingual Education.

Freinet, C. (1994). *Técnicas Freinet de la escuela moderna.* México DF: Siglo veintiuno editores, s.a. de c.v.

Freire, P. (1993). *Pedagogy of the oppressed* (3rd ed.). (Myra Bergman Ramos, Trans.). New York: Continuum Publishing.

Freire, P., & Macedo, D. (1987). *Literacy: Reading the word and the world.* Westport, CT: Bergin & Garvey.

Lee, E., Menkart, D., & Okazawa-Rey, M. (1998). *Beyond heroes and holidays: A practical guide to K–12 anti-racist, multicultural education and staff development.* Washington, DC: Network of Educators on the Americas.

McLaren, P. (1998). *Life in schools: An introduction to critical pedagogy in the foundations of education* (3rd ed.). New York: Addison Wesley Longman.

Nieto, S. (1992). *Affirming diversity: The sociopolitical context of multicultural education.* White Plains, NY: Longman.

Park, P. (1993). What is participatory research? A theoretical and methodological perspective. In P. Park, M. Brydon-Miller, B. Hall, & T. Jackson (Eds.), *Voices of change.* Westport, CT: Bergin & Garvey.

Temple, C., & Rodero, M. L. (1995). Reading around the world. *The Reading Teacher, 49* (2).

Walsh, C. (1991). *Pedagogy and the struggle for voice: Issue of language, power, and schooling for Puerto Ricans.* Westport, CT: Bergin & Garvey.

2

Approaches to Critical Literacy through Literature

MARY-LOUISE NEWLING

I can only say that education and schools ought to be about creating rather than destroying, about nurturing rather than abandoning, about taking the high road rather than the low road. If we do not take this high road, we will have effectively abandoned the most vulnerable of our children to the miserly mercies of those who see only threat and fearfulness in difference and diversity. If they do not know better, we do.
—AUGUST SCORNAIENCHI, RETIRED SUPERINTENDENT OF SCHOOLS, ALAMEDA COUNTY, CALIFORNIA

Literature Choices

Multicultural literature is big business these days, both because of the struggle by publishers to keep up with the demands of mostly urban teachers for literature that reflects the lives of their students, and also because of the firsthand experiences of some of these same teachers who have seen the difference in their students when they become engaged in a text that holds meaning for them, a point of reference that is familiar, an anchor in an otherwise scary and unstable school experience.

For mainstream U.S. students who are nonimmigrants, who are not refugees, who are not people of color, the choice of multicultural literature is every bit as important as it is for all students, but for different reasons. It is important that literature about European ethnicities be included in the choices of multicultural literature because to do so moves away from the mindset that Caucasian Americans have no culture, which is far from being the case. Inclusion also serves to eradicate the commonly held publishing belief that the Eurocentric experience does not have to be invoked as part of multicultural materials.

Historically, the stance has been to have a European curriculum and then to add multicultural materials as an adjunct. Demographics and world economies are changing so rapidly that it is important for all students to reflect on the fact that Whites are in the global minority, and that in places such as California, Whites are no longer the public school majority. Certainly, the White experience is part of the fabric of society and deserves to be included in the patchwork quilt, but it is no longer by any means the whole cloth. Global travel, international commerce, immigration patterns, and the Internet have seen to it that dealing with difference in an informed and sensitive fashion is a mandate for any knowledgeable citizenry of the twenty-first century.

How adept the nation's students become at dealing with difference and interacting with other human beings who do not look, speak, or act like them is an assignment that can be made or broken in the classrooms. It is a task that can succeed or fail, depending on what passes in schools for multicultural literature and multicultural education or the absence thereof.

Literature Selection Guidelines

The guidelines for selection of multilingual and multicultural materials are those that I employed when selecting resources for the Multilingual Multicultural Children's Literature Center, which I coordinated for five years, and when working with districts, schools, departments of teacher education, practicing teachers, and beginning teachers who are selecting materials for use with students. The guidelines I used are adapted in my own particular way, with my own judgment at the fore. The criteria themselves I adapted from the works of Beverly Slapin in *How to Tell the Difference: A Checklist for Evaluating Native American Children's Books* and *Through Indian Eyes: The Native Experience in Books for Children* and from Lyn Miller-Lachmann's *Our Family Our Friends Our World: An Annotated Guide to Significant Multicultural Books for Children and Teenagers.*

Teaching Strategies for Ethnic Studies and *Multicultural Education: Issues and Perspectives* by James and Carol Banks provide the theoretical framework for the rest of the work that I do in critical literacy for multicultural education. The visual aid of the computer (see Figure 2.1) provides a graphic representation of the immediately apparent (explicit) surface features of different cultures—such as clothing and food—as well as the more hidden (implicit) features—such as attitudes and behaviors.

Figure 2.1 illustrates that there are two levels of teaching about cultures. The first is the explicit—a superficial "heroes and holidays" celebrations level about which theorists caution educators. The second level, implicit, digs deeper to find values, perspectives, and worldviews—a more in-depth approach that leads to greater understanding. Indeed, it would be quite possible to wear a kimono every evening after work, eat burritos on a daily basis, and occupy a Yurt for many years without having any true inkling of the deeper manifestations of the cultures of Japan, Mexico, and Yugoslavia.

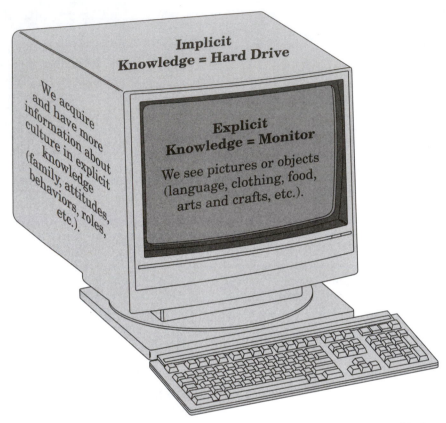

FIGURE 2.1   Computer Program Demonstrating Explicit and Implicit Knowledge

Languages Reflect the Community

As the computer graphic indicates, language is one of the more readily apparent features of a culture. A collection of multilingual and multicultural literature should therefore be available in different languages, as reflected by the linguistic realities of community. This includes books in the primary language as well as books in translation. The issues of appropriateness, accuracy of translations, as well as what gets translated are important, highly charged political questions, but are beyond the scope of this chapter.

Considerations When Selecting Multicultural Books

The driving force behind any good collection of multicultural literature includes the following:

- Books and materials must reflect the implicit or less readily obvious aspects of different cultures. These include values, family structure, religion, group organization, systems of government, and gender and age concerns.
- It is the purpose of any good collection of multicultural literature to present the people of the culture going about their everyday business, doing what they do within the dictates of their culture.
- It is of paramount importance to remember that there is no one Hmong experience, no one Vietnamese experience, no single Cuban or Puerto Rican experience. Just as there are multiple variations of the lives of members of the U.S. mainstream, so too are there multifaceted, divergent experiences among members of the same cultural and linguistic groups here in the United States.

Choosing Appropriate Books of Study

The realm of multicultural literature is one that is studded with much heated debate about what is good and what is not good. Multicultural literature for children and young adults is by no means exempt from the heat generated in this discourse. There are seven main criteria that can be used to select multicultural literature. In addition to these, all the elements that make up a gripping story and that capture the interest of the reader should also be present.

Criteria for Selection

1. *General accuracy* is the first hallmark of good multicultural literature for children and young adults. Is the story factual? This is an issue with books coming into the United States from places

such as the Philippines and the Caribbean. Often, some elements of the culture are sanitized to appeal to a U.S. readership. Many of the books written for young readers in the English-speaking Caribbean would not sit well with a U.S. reading public because of what would be deemed sexist or inappropriate language in the U.S. context. An example is Trinidadian author Michael Anthony's *Green Days by the River,* where a young boy, Shell, is attacked by the dogs of his girlfriend's father as a warning not to get too close to his daughter. Added to that is the fact that the dogs have been fed Dragon's Blood, a substance that makes urination very painful, thus ensuring that they are mean, angry, and all the more eager to attack Shell. This book, although extremely popular with adolescent boys in the English-speaking Caribbean, would undoubtedly raise a few eyebrows in the United States.

Harper Lee's *To Kill a Mockingbird* continues to attract controversy yet is still on many core literature lists in school districts, being touted as African American literature, or literature about the Black experience. It is really neither of those things. *To Kill a Mockingbird* is the story of Atticus Finch, his children, Boo Radley, and the people of Maycomb County. The Black people in the book, more often than not, are referred to by racial epithets and exist as mere shadows, rather than as well-developed characters. Even the character of Tom Robinson, the accused, is never developed. His main purpose in the book is to develop the character of Atticus Finch, liberal lawyer. Calpurnia the maid is the archetype of the Mammy figure, and the other Black characters in the book are shadows hovering in the background. The final message of the book is that Tom Robinson's life might have been saved if only he had faith in the legal system and waited for Atticus to stage a retrial. Tom Robinson is presented as a victim through and through. *To Kill a Mockingbird* is the story of Atticus Finch, gentle father, liberal lawyer, and all around good guy. Multicultural literature it is not, nor does it even pretend to be about the Black experience other than as glimpses of Black characters presented merely as backdrop and for plot advancement. It upsets many people when I say this in presentations about *To Kill a Mockingbird.* Many people have fond memories of the book and have been teaching it for years.

2. *Stereotyping* is also a very important issue to consider when selecting multicultural literature. Books such as *The House That Crack Built* and *Life in the Ghetto* perpetuate images of African Americans strung out on drugs and living in substandard housing. These books can be contrasted to the deeper, far more realistic books of Candy Dawson Boyd, which look at various sectors of the African American class structure in all its complexity, as do the books of Virginia Hamilton and Walter Dean Myers. In many instances, Native Americans have also been paid a great disservice by what has been published. The use of the past tense and the depiction of many Native peoples as historical figures gives rise to the misinformation that the genocide of Native Americans has been complete, which is very far from being the case. Sherman Alexie and Joseph Bruchac are two Native American writers whose books have proven popular with junior high and high school readers and whose work does much to portray the lives of urban Native Americans today.

3. *Language* is another key consideration in the selection of literature for children and adolescents. If there are passages of culturally specific language in the book, Ebonics or otherwise, it is very important that they be structurally accurate renditions of the language of the speakers. *The Cay* is a big offender in this regard, as it fails dismally at an approximation of the speech of the Curaçao natives. Equally appalling and insulting are the linguistic attempts of *Indian in the Cupboard* and *Sign of the Beaver,* in which Native Americans are made to speak what Beverly Slapin so aptly terms "Early Jawbreaker."

4. *Author's authenticity* is one of the key questions that arises sooner rather than later regarding the background of the person writing the book. There are those critics who feel that only persons who are of the culture should write the books. These persons ascribe to the Emic, or insider, perspective body of thought. Others belong to the Etic, or outsider, perspective and for these persons the most important fact is that the author be able to write with enough sensitivity and empathy as if he or she were a member of the culture. I fall into the second group, but having said that, I feel that it is important to examine why the book has been written in the first place.

David Frost Introduces Trinidad and Tobago is a fine surface introduction to the two islands that I call home. The book is good for tourists, good for intending visitors to the islands, and good even as a reference for locals. However, if I were in search of a book that spoke of the humor, the character, and the complexities of the place, I would certainly not find it with David Frost. Frost is not party to the jokes, the insider information, nor the local flavors and hues. However, he has done his homework; the book is well researched, accurate, and lives up to its purpose as a piece of tourist information.

A good rule of thumb with authors who are writing about cultures other than their own is to check and see if the authors have done their homework. What qualifies the author to write about Kenya from the persona of a Kenyan, or about Cambodia from the viewpoint of a young refugee boy? Sometimes what emerges is a documentary piece rather than a work of multicultural literature, as in the case of Eve Bunting's *Smoky Night,* which documents a fictional event in the aftermath of the Los Angeles riots, but goes no deeper than that. Sometimes the result is an exotic setting for an adventure story. This is true of a work such as Frances Temple's *A Taste of Salt,* ostensibly set in Haiti.

In order to illustrate the difference in style and tone between insider and outsider perspectives, it is useful to juxtapose a reading of Temple's *A Taste of Salt* with a reading of Haitian writer Edwidge Danticat's *Breath, Eyes and Memory,* a story of the author's childhood in Haiti and her move to the United States. Danticat's entire frame of reference is Haitian: her syntax, her easy acquaintance with the characters, and her deeply conveyed fear of the Tonton Macoutes, the strongmen of the Duvalier regime. Temple's book, on the other hand, reads like what it is—an adventure story in an exotic setting. If an editor were to do a global computer search and delete all references to Haiti and things Haitian, inserting instead Jamaica, or Belize, or any tropical country where there has been political unrest, the story would remain pretty much as it is. It is and would remain an adventure story in a tropical, politically troubled setting, but hardly considered multicultural literature. The same is true of Eve Bunting's *Smoky Night*. This Caldecott Award–winning book documents the Los Angeles looting and rioting in a fictionalized way. The tone is that of the TV cameraperson commenting as the footage of events appear. There is no attempt at historical context, no social commentary, just documentation. At the end of the story, the message of the Korean family cat and the African American family cat is a highly simplistic "Can't we all get along?" To her credit, Bunting is one of the few children's book authors to have attempted to fictionalize the Los Angeles riots, but a deeper look at the phenomenon of race relations is required for classroom fare. For a far more gripping account of a riot and its aftermath, I strongly recommend June Jordan's essay, "Letter to Michael," in her collection of essays entitled *Moving towards Home*.

5. *Balance and multidimensionality* in the selection of quality multicultural literature for children and adolescents is another key issue. In a book such as *Juanita Fights the School Board,* part of the Roosevelt High trilogy, Juanita does not come lightly to her decision to challenge her expulsion from school. The reader is able to share Juanita's vacillation, her fear and her internal struggles with herself as she finally summons up the courage to appear in front of the school board on her own behalf. The same is true of Zee Edgell's *Beka Lamb*. This novel of adolescence, set in Belize, deals with the turmoil of a young girl who falls madly in love with her boyfriend, a handsome young student, only to have him jilt her once he finds out that she is pregnant.

6. *The integration of cultural information* is another key hallmark of quality multicultural literature. In Danny Santiago's *Famous All over Town,* the Mexican American culture is part of what the young protagonist must grapple with as he sees his family disintegrating. The illusion of the nuclear family begins to crumble, the ideal father/mother bond dissipates before his eyes, and his sister's actions are outside the realm of cultural expectations for a young Mexican American girl. The cultural manifestations are woven into the story as part of the lives of the characters, which is just the way they should be.

Laurence Yep's *Child of the Owl* deals with similar themes about changes within a family, this time from a young girl's perspective. The images of Chinatown are real, part of the story, and integrated into the young protagonist's growing awareness of herself and of the importance of her Chinese grandmother in her life. Also highly recommended is Yep's autobiographical piece, *The Lost Garden*.

7. *Illustrations* are generally of less pivotal concern in books for older readers, but still an issue. Many children's books are appropriate for classroom use with older readers, and even with adults. For example, the visuals of *The Village of Round and Square Houses* would be very appropriate to introduce a book such as Nigerian novelist Chinua Achebe's *Things Fall Apart*. This is also true of the book or video presentation of the Anansi tale, *A Story, A Story*. Well worth mentioning, too, are two children's books: Carmen Lomas Garza's *Family Pictures,* now currently available in big book format, and Bobbi Salinas's *The Three Pigs: Nacho, Tito and Miguel*. Both of these books have exquisite visuals that provide excellent, accurate, and politically savvy windows into Mexican American culture and can clearly function as introductions to Mexican American writings for older readers such as *The House on Mango Street* and *Famous All over Town*. It is important that the illustrations be accurate, be up to date, and stay clear of stereotyping. Captions to photographs should be specific to time and place rather than merely stating, "A Village in Asia" or "A Seaside Town in Europe."

Books are expensive, and multicultural literature books are no exception. It is useful for the classroom teacher and the discerning school librarian or library teacher to have an idea of what is of high quality in order to stock those items in the school library. Again, there has been such a plethora of poor quality, mediocre, and downright racist and substandard multicultural books that it is a great relief to recognize that there is also a whole lot of very high quality work written by authors of varying cultures. All children deserve the very best, and we are fortunate to be able to give it to them as the improvements in multicultural publishing continue to happen.

Reflections

It is expected that each teacher will make changes and adaptations as required to meet the needs and interests of their students. Demographics are rapidly changing, literacy levels and test scores of immigrant students and children of color continue to be of concern to educators. In the rush for political power, more than ever one is finding politicians making decisions about education, with no educators at the discussion tables. Teaching is a profession, a vocation. We teachers have a moral responsibility to prepare students to assume control over their lives, to reach their greatest potential. We can make a difference to their school experience, to the type of informed citizenry that this country needs. There is an Afghan proverb that states, "The dog barks, but the caravan moves on." Our students live their lives, they move on, and more students come. We can make a difference or we can be as barking dogs, giving voice into the void long after the camels have left the desert.

Using Literature for Dealing with Sensitive Issues in the Classroom

When I was a classroom teacher, I worked in an elementary school during the day and taught in an adult school at night. I did this for many years, paying my way through graduate school. In the adult school, I had very few *adult* students. Most of them were high school students who, for one reason or another, did not have enough credits and needed to take night classes to be able to graduate with their peers. Their reasons for attending night school were varied—some were teen mothers, others had serious absentee problems, some had been on probation, others were out of the system for disciplinary reasons.

Many of my students were people of color, mostly Latino and African American, a few were obviously gay and had been emotionally mangled by their high school experiences. I learned a lot about my students through their creative writings and their journal entries. One summer session, I had a particularly low-achieving class. They seemed particulary reluctant to be there, and lacked all motivation. I decided to spark their interest by using a statistical article that *Time Magazine* had recently published about the high dropout rates of African American and Latino youths. The article went on to cite statistics and numbers of school dropouts.

To date, my bringing that article to class and my attempt to use it as a teaching tool was the worst miscalculation of my teaching career. My students were outraged. They accused me of having brought in the article to put them down. Had I made up the article? Had I written it? After I managed to calm things down somewhat, I decided that I would teach only basics and grammar, nothing that might stir them to volatile reaction. I was determined to see the semester to the end. The hot summer evenings wore on. My class limped along, not going badly, but certainly not going well. Then the due date for the first book report rolled along. Gerry, one of my quieter students, was absent on the date the assignment was due. "I'll get it from him on Wednesday," I thought. But for Gerry, Wednesday never came. He had been arrested on murder charges. An argument had gone wrong, heated words had been flung, and racial slurs exchanged. At the end of it, Latino Gerry stood with a smoking gun over the body of a 20-year-old African American acquaintance of his. I knew then that I had to address the deeper issues that were facing my students. I also felt a moral obligation to help my students grapple with the dizzying and often terrifying changes that were going on in their lives. I knew better than to try factual articles, but I wondered if I could get my point across through literature. This was the birth of my thematic units dealing with sensitive issues.

Thematic Units: Approaches to Critical Literacy

I wanted to begin the session with a selection of literature that dealt with a sensitive issue—in this case, the topic of racial prejudice—but in a manner that my students would not find incendiary or threatening. I decided to work with one of Nigerian Nobel prizewinner Wole Soyinka's early poems, "Telephone Conversation." It is set in London, where Soyinka was a graduate student, and deals with the male protagonist's difficulties in renting an apartment. The poem is in two voices, that of the African male tenant to be and that of the White female landlady. My students responded very well to the poem and did not seem at all deterred by some of the very British expressions and references. We read it aloud several times in class, discussing the meaning, and then they were ready for the point-of-view writing assignment.

The Process
Students were numbered off in pairs of 1s and 2s. The 1s were assigned to write about the experience from the perspective of the tenant; the 2s were to write from the landlady's point of view. After the assignment was completed, a number 1 would pair up with a number 2 and they would read their pieces to each other. The opposing point of view was assigned as a follow-up assignment. Finally, the students were asked to reflect on the experiences of the point-of-view writing in their own journals. I eventually began to feel that we were making some progress toward grappling with some deeper issues.

Golden Lines

I then chose to look at the issue of primary language loss and did this through Tove Skutnabb-Kangas's translation of Theodor Kallifatides's poem, "My Language and I." This was read in conjunction with Alma Flor Ada's, *My Name Is Maria Isabel,* which deals with a teacher anglicizing a Latina child's name. This is an example of using younger children's literature with older students. My students were then given a cross-section of short readings about the issues of languages and cultures. These included excerpts from *The Autobiography of Malcolm X* and *The House on Mango Street,* selections of student stories from *Through Our Eyes,* an excerpt from *The Autobiography of Angela Davis,* a selection from Laurence Yep's *The Lost Garden,* and one from Maxine Hong Kingston's *The Woman Warrior.*

The Process

Students were asked to read one selection each, to group themselves according to similar articles, and to take responsibility for
sharing the gist of the article with the rest of the class. Each student
in the group was asked to highlight a "golden paragraph," one that
was especially well written or relevant to his or her experience. As
a follow-up, each student was asked to write his or her own cultural
and linguistic autobiography and to share it with a classmate. The
other student would then underline the golden paragraph (or line)
and read it to the class, taking turns.

Venn Diagrams for Comparing and Contrasting

The topics of class issues and within-group differences were treated
by a compare/contrast type of activity using Francisco Jimenez's,
"The Circuit," and Sandra Cisneros's, "Eleven," taken from *Woman
Hollering Creek,* and an excerpt from Angela Davis's autobiography
where, in reference to a childhood incident, she talks of the difference in treatment meted out to her and her sister. The incident
takes place in a shoe store in segregated Birmingham, Alabama,
when they are mistaken for French-speaking West Indians as
opposed to African Americans. An effective comparison and con-
trast of the issues in any two excerpts works well using a Venn diagram. A connection between student and literature was then made
by asking students to write about a time when they acted in an
unfair or unjust manner toward someone because he or she was different. Sharing of this piece of writing was voluntary.

Interactive Partner Duologs

The theme of gender orientation may be introduced via a piece of
nonfiction. This can be done through an editorial that weighs the
pros and cons of addressing the issue of gender orientation in
schools. Using a structure called *interactive partner duologs,* students are numbered off by twos and are assigned a point of view on
the issue. They are asked to write an argument from their stand-
point, and then at a later time they are assigned the opposing view-

point. This activity acts as a precursor to reading selections of gay and lesbian literature, such as *From the Notebooks of Melanin Sun,* and anthologies, such as *Two Teenagers in Twenty* and *Growing up Gay in America.* I am very aware that a teacher is taking a risk in dealing with gay/lesbian issues in the classroom. If this is a choice the teacher makes, sending a letter home to parents outlining the syllabus at the beginning of the term is one way of allowing parents to give their input. It is also a good idea to share these plans with the principal or supervisor. I firmly believe that to address issues of diversity and difference at one level and not at others is to do a great disservice to all students as well as gay and lesbian ones.

Additional Suggestions for Multicultural Curriculum

Literature circles can involve activities using the following books that reflect different cultures and ethnic groups: *The Sunita Experiment* (East Indian), *Child of the Owl* (Chinese), *The Lost Garden* (Chinese), *Journey to Topaz* (Japanese), *Nobody's Family Is Going to Change* (African American), *Famous All over Town* (Mexican American), and *Slake's Limbo* (European American).

The principle behind literature circles is that all students will eventually read all the books. In the preceding circle, for example, the group doing *The Sunita Experiment* would next move to *Child of the Owl,* then to *The Lost Garden,* and so on, until all books have been read.

The instructor works with each group for part of each session, engaging in active discussion and interaction about the reading. Each group is accountable every day. Possible assignments include interactive literature logs, sociograms (symbolic story representations either as scale models, drawings, or character or plot maps), partial book reports (where students select some of the questions), full book reports, interviews with the author, and dramatization of parts of the book. Students tell their own family stories, illustrating them with family pictures. Some students may not be comfortable with bringing family photographs to school; this issue can be dealt with sensitively on an individual basis. Other ideas include:

- Dramatize folktales.
- Read folktales of different ethnicities.
- Create comic strips based on folktales.
- Have students bring in proverbs from home, both in their primary languages and in English. Assign them to find equivalents in different cultures. Do the same for folktales.
- Have students illustrate/make posters of their proverbs and folktales.
- Look at folktales across cultures—for example, Cinderella stories exist in many different cultures.
- Read articles about people of different ethnicities, taking care to select positive role models, and some who are still alive. Not all African Americans are sports or entertainment personalities. Suggestions include Laurence Yep (author), Malcolm X (civil rights activist), Angela Davis (civil rights activist), Mother Teresa (social worker), Indira Ghandi (former prime minister of India), Wilma Mankiller (head of the Cherokee Nation), César Chavez (social activist), and Dolores Huerta (social activist).
- Have students interview an older relative about somebody whom they consider to be a hero/heroine of their culture.

References

Banks, J. (1997). *Teaching strategies for ethnic studies.* Boston: Allyn and Bacon.

Banks, J., & Banks, C. (Eds.). (1989). *Multicultural education: Issues and perspectives.* Boston: Allyn and Bacon.

Greenfield, E. (1989). Writing for children, a joy and a responsibility. In *The Black American in books for children.* Metchuen, NJ: Scarecrow Books.

Miller-Lachmann, L. (1992). *Our family our friends our world: An annotated guide to significant multicultural books for children and teenagers.* New Providence, NJ: R. R. Bowker.

Skutnabb-Kangas, T. (1988). *Minority education: From shame to struggle.* Clevedon, England: Multilingual Matters.

Slapin, B., & Seale, D. (Eds.). (1992). *Through Indian eyes: The Native experience in books for children.* Philadelphia: New Society Publishers.

Bibliography of Books for Older Readers

Adler, C. S. (1995). *Youn Hee & me.* New York: Harcourt Brace. **Korean.**

Baillie, Allan. (1992). *Little brother.* New York: Puffin. **Cambodian.**

Bode, Janet. (1989). *New kids in town.* New York: Scholastic. **Immigrants.**

Bruchac, Joseph. (1993). *Flying with the eagle, racing the great bear.* Bridgewater Books. **Native American.**

Callaway, Sydney, & Witherspoon, Gary. (1974). *Grandfather stories of the Navajos.* AZ: Rough Rock Press. **Navajo.**

Cisneros, Sandra. (1989). *The house on Mango Street.* New York: Vintage. **Mexican American.**

Crane Wartski, Maureen. (1980). *A long way from home.* New York: Signet. **Vietnamese.**

Crew, Linda. (1989). *Children of the river.* New York: Laurel Leaf. **Cambodian.**

David, Jay. (1992). *Growing up black.* New York: Avon. **African American.**

Dawson Boyd, Candy. (1987). *Charlie Pippin.* New York: Puffin. **African American.**

Douglass, Frederick. (1968). *Narrative of the life of Frederick Douglass.* New York: Signet. **African American.**

Fitzhugh, Louise. (1991). *Nobody's family is going to change.* New York: Farrar, Straus & Giroux. **African American.**

García Marquez, Gabriel. (1983). *Chronicle of a death foretold.* New York: Knopf. **Colombian.**

Garden, Nancy. (1994). *Annie on my mind.* New York: Farrar, Straus & Giroux. **Gay/Lesbian.**

Giovanni, Nikki. (Ed.). (1994). *Grandmothers.* New York: Henry Holt. **African American.**

Gogol, Sara. (1992). *Vatsana's lucky new year.* New York: Lerner. **Lao.**

Greenberg Baker, Carin. (1992). *Girl trouble.* New York: Puffin. **Vietnamese.**

Grossman, Sari. (Ed.). (1995). *In a new land.* Lincoln, IL: National Textbook. **Immigrants.**

Guy, Rosa. (1992). *The friends.* New York: Bantam. **Caribbean/USA.**

Heron, Ann. (1994). *Two teenagers in twenty.* Boston: Alyson Publications. **Gay/Lesbian.**

Hodge, Merle. (1994). *For the life of Laetitia.* New York: Farrar, Straus & Giroux. **Trinidadian.**

Johnson, Charles. (Ed.). (1992). *Myths, legends and folk tales from the Hmong of Laos.* St. Paul, MN: Macalester College. **Hmong.**

López, Tiffany Ana. (Ed.). (1993). *Growing up Chicana/o.* New York: William Morrow. **Chicano/Mexican American.**

Mazer, Anne. (Ed.). (1994). *Going where I'm coming from.* New York: Persea Books. **Immigrants.**

Mills, Claudia. (1981). *Luisa's American.* New York: Four Winds Press. **Cuban American.**

Morris, Mervyn. (Ed.). (1990). *The Faber book of contemporary Caribbean short stories.* London: Faber. **Caribbean.**

Myers, Walter Dean. (1984). *Motown and Didi.* New York: Laurel Leaf. **African American.**

Riley, Patricia. (Ed.). (1995). *Growing up Native American.* New York: Avon. **Native American.**

Rochman, Hazel. (Ed.). (1990). *Somehow tenderness survives.* New York: Harper Trophy. **South African.**

Rochman, Hazel, & McCampbell, Darlene Z. (Eds.). (1997). *Leaving home stories.* New York: HarperCollins. **Multicultural Collection.**

Santiago, Danny. (1984). *Famous all over town.* New York: Plume. **Mexican American.**

Soto, Gary. (1990). *Baseball in April and other stories.* San Diego: Harcourt Brace. **Mexican American.**

Sterling, Shirley. (1993). *My name is Seepeetza.* Toronto: Douglas & McIntyre. **Salish Nation.**

Velásquez, Gloria. (1994). *Juanita fights the school board.* Houston: Piñata Books. **Mexican American.**

Velásquez, Gloria. (1995). *Maya's divided world.* Houston: Piñata Books. **Mexican American.**

Velásquez, Gloria. (1996). *Tommy stands alone.* Houston: Piñata Books. **Mexican American.**

Wheeler, Jordan. (1989). *Brothers in arms.* Winnipeg, Manitoba: Pemmican. **Native American.**

Woodson, Jacqueline. (Ed.). (1996). *A way out of no way.* New York: Henry Holt. **African American.**

Yep, Laurence. (1990). *Child of the owl.* New York: HarperCollins. **Chinese American.**

Yep, Laurence. (1991). *The lost garden.* New York: Julian Messner. **Chinese American.**

Zobel, Joseph. (1980). *Black shack alley.* London: Heinemann. **Martiniquan.**

3

Breaking through the Culture of Silence

ROSARIO DÍAZ-GREENBERG

> *If my teachers realized the amount of information that each of us have, they would give us the time to express our feelings about our cultures, families, and personal histories. This would lead to a better understanding among students and would foster communication rather than separation between groups.* —HIGH SCHOOL STUDENT

Transformative theorists have argued that educators and students must be aware of the causes, existence, and effects of the hidden curriculum in order to critically analyze it and make it work toward the total development of young people. Although I am aware that this is not a simple task, the work I have done with my students at the high school level convinces me that it can be done. As critical educators, it is important that we look at different aspects of education within the school and denounce practices that serve only the interests of a few.

In the fall of 1991, I had the opportunity to work as a researcher and a teacher with a group of young Latino suburban high school students. Together, we attempted to define our own identity and reclaim our voices. I learned that coming to voice is essential if we are to change the conditions of subordination and suppression felt by students. Students' reflections spoke to the structured silence they feel exists within the educational system and their communities resulting in the silencing of voice. The following narration describes three particular areas affecting student achievement and advancement: teacher/student interaction and its impact on student achievement, the role of the hidden curriculum, and the consequent absence of dialogue. The second part of the chapter describes the approach I used to break through the culture of silence.

Teacher/Student Interaction

The analysis of teacher/student interaction has been the subject of a great deal of research for over 30 years. Most of the studies concentrate on the amount of time a teacher spends questioning, praising, or correcting students. Unfortunately, many studies reveal that teachers praise low achievers less often, criticize them more frequently, and allow them less opportunity to answer questions and less time to respond (Good, 1987). Silberman (1970) adds to these findings that in most classrooms it is the teacher who does most of the talking.

In 1971, the U.S. Commission on Civil Rights presented its findings based on a study of 400 classrooms, including Mexican American students. This study found that in only two types of interaction do Latino children receive more attention than other students—giving directions and criticizing. The report also documents the following facts: In the areas of development of ideas, praise, and positive response, teachers engaged Mexican American students approximately 40 percent less often than Eurocentric students. Similarly, teachers asked questions from Latino students 21 percent less often than they did from Eurocentric students.

Another study carried out over a six-year period with 97 bilingual and monolingual classrooms containing Latino students suggests a buildup of negative attitudes toward Latino children by teachers who failed to include these children in activities and who avoided interaction and eye contact with them. When Latino students disproved the teachers' expectations of their ability, the teachers often acted in a resentful and suspicious manner (Ortiz, 1988).

In 1992, the American Association of University Women (AAUW) reported that teachers often treat minority students and Eurocentric students differently. This lack of positive teacher/student interaction addresses a salient concern that transformative educators seek to dismantle through the use of critical literacy. A need exists to change an underlying structure within the traditional school model often considered the cause for the negative attitudes existing between teacher and student.

Teacher Expectations and Student Achievement

The academic achievement of students appears to be directly affected by teachers' expectations (Smey-Richman, 1989). The expectations that a teacher has of his or her students are deeply influenced by the socioeconomic characteristics of each student (Darder, 1991).

Rosenthal and Jacobson's Pygmalion experiment (1968), perhaps the best known and most replicated study in this area, intended to show that if teachers raise their expectations on students' intellectual ability, the students' achievement will increase. Rubovits and Maehr (1973) replicated the Rosenthal and Jacobson study to observe the effects of teachers' expectations on the performance of African American and Eurocentric students. They noted that Eurocentric students were given preferential and more encouraging treatment over African American students, who were often ignored. Similar findings were reported by Cornbleth and Korth in 1980.

The Hidden Curriculum

A large body of literature speaks to what has become known as the *hidden curriculum,* which Giroux (1983) defines as "those norms, values, and beliefs embedded in and transmitted to students through the underlying rules that structure the routines and social relationships in schools and classroom life" (p. 47). Traditional education understands the concept of hidden curriculum as a construct of climate, unspoken words, and actions that are part of the transmission model (Jackson, 1968). The transformative theorists see the hidden curriculum as a set of values of the status quo being covertly imposed on students.

Palmer (1983) adds his thoughts on the hidden curriculum as perpetuating the passive role of the students: Without being allowed to examine, reflect, and act on transforming the socioeconomic forces that shape their destiny, students of color repeat the vicious cycle of violence and poverty that exists in their surroundings, thus perpetuating the self-fulfilling prophesy of academic failure.

Focus of study is placed on the conduct, cultural values, and beliefs that exist within the dominant school groups, leaving the inner-self unexamined. By excluding views of ethnic and cultural groups not considered the mainstream, the hidden curriculum constitutes a barrier or a means of isolation, creating an atmosphere of exclusion and marginalization.

The Absence of Dialogue

Understanding the importance of dialogue used in the classroom necessitates a discussion about the differences between dialogue and conversation or verbal interaction. Although this study focuses on *dialogue,* a very specific form of interaction, it bears noting that U.S. classrooms lack *conversation.* The absence of verbal interaction between teachers and students has been carefully scrutinized by Goodlad (1984), Silberman (1970), and Sizer (1984), among others. Teacher talk dominates instructional time. Goodlad (1984) found that most talk emanates from teacher to students, and does not allow student talk to occur. On average, approximately 75 percent of class time was spent on instruction. Of that time, 70 percent flowed as "talk" from teacher to students. Goodlad also noted that teachers outtalked the entire class of students by a ratio of three to one.

In a similar study, Silberman (1970) found teacher-centered classroom environments predominating, with teachers telling and questioning and children responding individually or in chorus. In these surroundings, children learn to assume a passive role within the classroom in order to succeed. By dominating the classroom, most teachers allow students no option except passivity.

In 1984, Sizer reported that within the U.S. classroom dialogue was almost nonexistent. Similarly, Ramirez (1991) found in his national bilingual study that in over half of the interactions that teachers have with students, students do not produce any language, since they are only listening. This lack of verbal interaction or conversation within the classroom tends to exacerbate the covert conditions that lead to the absence of dialogue.

The absence of dialogue, or what Poplin (1991, p. 33) calls "the paucity of language experienced by students," in the classroom relates to the excessive use of "frontal teaching" or teacher-controlled talk. Freire (cited in Galeano, 1973, p. 288) hypothesized that absence of dialogue leads students to immerse themselves into the culture of silence where they are led "to absorb an alien, desiccated, sterile memory fabricated by the oppressor, so that they will resign themselves to a life that isn't theirs as if it were the only one possible."

The Culture of Silence

In some instances, students become silent "because they no longer expect education to include the joy of learning, moments of passion, or inspiration, or comedy" (Shor & Freire, 1987, p. 122). The affective domain no longer presides in the classroom. Eradicated by the need to concentrate on other aspects of education, it allows the teacher to exercise control. Observing this situation, Goodlad (1984) concluded that many teachers opt to maintain a flat emotional tone as a means to control the class, thereby curtailing exuberance, abrasiveness, and praise. Developing an emotional flatness subtracts from the affective domain and adds to the conditions that foster passivity and resistance on the part of students, submerging them in the culture of silence.

Breaking the Silence

Ever since I was little, my parents told me that my teachers were people I could go to for advice and talk to if my mother or father were not there. The teachers were supposed to take my parents' place for part of the day. Having this in mind, I supposed that my teachers would recognize and appreciate my beliefs, background, and culture. Unfortunately, it is not like that at all.—HIGH SCHOOL STUDENT

In working with my students, I found the suggestions included in *Parents and Children as Authors and Protagonists: A Critical Pedagogy Approach to Home-School Interaction* (Ada, 1992) contributing to positive changes in my students' motivational success and interest levels. The model I explain demonstrates what can happen when students are given an opportunity to research their families' past and share it in the classroom. The students learn what it means to establish an internal dialogue and how to increase communication between members of their family. The results fostered an increase in home/school interaction and parent/child communication.

The Students' Voices

"As students become aware of the tremendous discrepancy existing between what the school proposes as accepted models of conduct and behavior and what they themselves have experienced so far at home, there [is] a . . . conflict" (Ada, 1992, p. 47). An example of this issue is expressed in the following writing:

> *In the format of schools and study in society today the connection between the home and the school has been lost. Few teachers encourage their students to really find out about what goes on in the minds of their parents. In this light, the students create a gap between themselves and their families. This is especially true for families of foreign origin such as Hispanic families. As the younger generations grow up they pull away from the culture of their parents. . . . This is why it is imperative that the students are encouraged to go home and talk with the family . . . to find out about their culture and tradition.—HIGH SCHOOL SENIOR*

Also, students become aware of the fact that "the curriculum in no way incorporates or even acknowledges the knowledge of the parents and the richness of the home culture . . . [thus] creating a negative self image" (Ada, 1992, p. 47). This student's writing clearly exemplifies the latter:

> *I have never had a class that has allowed me to take pride in who I am, or a teacher who has even cared to find out about my family, but I would appreciate having this opportunity.*
> *—HIGH SCHOOL SOPHOMORE*

However, if the school attempts to incorporate "the knowledge that the parents or primary caretakers of children have" (Ada, 1992, p. 48) a different situation happens:

> *School is a fine place to learn about material things but if you incorporate what you learn from your family and what you know from your heritage, it becomes a greater learning experience.—HIGH SCHOOL JUNIOR*

The voices of these students invite educators to reflect on the importance of establishing a connection between the home and the school. As teachers, we are constantly searching for new approaches to education that can allow us to reach our students and enrich their lives. Often, we overlook the obvious and do not take into consideration the wealth of information that our students and their families already possess. By attempting to involve the students and their families in the learning process, we begin to validate their culture and home-based experiences, thus offering them an opportunity to "share their multiple forms of knowledge" (Ada, 1992, p. 49) with each other and the members of the school community.

The Process: Breaking the Silence

The following chronological account explains the steps followed in my classroom in order to establish a connection between the parents and the school. It also describes the effect this process had on those involved in terms of increasing self-esteem, fostering communication between parents and children, and increasing home/school interaction. (A summary of the stages of development in "breaking the silence" appears in Figure 3.1.)

1. *First Connections: Taking a Survey*
The purpose of this survey was to begin a communication process between the home and the school by inviting the parents to share their home-based experiences with the teacher, thus making "an authentic effort to include parents in the education of their children" (Ada, 1992, p. 48). Over 75 percent of the parents responded within the next three days.

Using the information provided, we were able to make graphs and charts showing how many countries were represented by the students, how many people came from each country, what items their parents liked about the community, and what advice the parents had for the children. The students began to create knowledge and "name the world" (Freire, 1970, p. 77) by tapping into their parents' and grandparents' existing knowledge and becoming "co-investigators in looking together at their reality" (Ada, 1992, p. 49).

Some 80 percent of the parents wrote about the importance of staying in school and obtaining a good education in order to succeed

FIGURE 3.1   Breaking the Silence: The Stages of Development (a chronological account of the process leading to establishing a connection between the parents and the school)

Phase I: *First* *Connections*	**Taking a Survey** Students were asked to take a survey home that included basic questions: name and place of origin, what they liked about their community, what they missed most about leaving their other community, what kind of advice they had for their children, and so on. *Purpose:* Opening the communication process between the home and school begins by inviting parents and students to share their home-based experiences. A newsletter was written that included various comments of students and parents. Included was a short biography of the teacher.
Phase II: *Guiding the* *Dialogue*	**Developing a Questionnaire** Using Ada's Creative Reading Approach, the students, with the teacher guiding the process, wrote a set of 14 questions, which were used to interview the parents. *Purpose:* This step is important in establishing a dialogue between the children and their parents.
Phase III: *Reflection*	**Reflecting on the Experience** The contents of their questionnaires they wrote with their parents were shared with each other and with a partner. The reflections were jointly and individually reflected. *Purpose:* The information collected is part of the students' lived experience. Dialogue and reflection lead them to understand their life experiences and their family, and, most important, it cannot be generalized to fit the group.
Phase IV: *Validation* *and the* *Creative* *Process*	**Becoming Authors** Expanding on the information obtained during the interviews, the students were asked to author a book with their parents. Students were guided through the steps.

in life. This information was very important because it showed how many Hispanic parents considered education as the most important aspect in their children's lives. Several parents wrote comments saying how this was the first time a teacher ever asked questions about the family and how much it meant to share their views with the children and the rest of the class. One of the most moving testimonies came from a girl who had recently arrived in the United States to live with her father for the first time. She wrote, "Before this activity I hardly knew who my father was. I did not know him as a person. We did not have anything to talk about." Her father enjoyed the activity and wrote a note stating, "Thank you for providing this activity. I hope you will continue doing this type of work with us."

2. *The Teacher Shares Self with the Parents: Writing an Autobiography*
Realizing how important the activity had been to us, I decided to follow it by writing a short autobiography that was included in our newsletter. This was one way of sharing oneself with the students' families in order to strengthen the home/school interaction process. Writing about myself made me realize how much it meant to be willing to share my personal life with my students and their parents and how much I was asking of the parents and relatives.

After reading the newsletter in class, the students were asked to take it home and read it with their families. The parents' reaction was very positive. Several of them had gone through similar experiences and shared them with us in writing: "I too went to the same kind of school when I first came to the United States."

It was at this point that the students began to see me as an individual. This was very important because it meant that I was no longer the figure of authority, but another human being who had had to overcome many of the same problems they were having in their lives. Thus we began "reconciling both poles of the contradiction so that both became simultaneously teachers and students" (Freire, 1970, p. 59).

3. *The Rudiments of Voice: Developing a Questionnaire*
Using the descriptive, personal interpretive, critical analysis and creative action phases as described in Ada's Creative Reading

Approach (see Chapter 7), we wrote a set of 14 questions, which were used to interview the parents. This step was meant to establish a dialogue between the children and their parents by having them engage in a question and answer process. One parent wrote, "For the past seven years we were not able to discuss the reasons why we had to leave our own country. This interview gave us a chance to open up and talk about it." A student stated, "Many times my parents are too busy to sit down to talk. However, by doing the interview, they had a chance to tell me about my ancestors whom they had never discussed with me before."

4. *Becoming Authors and Protagonists: Children Authoring Books about Their Parents*

The most important part of this project took place when the students began writing biographical books. Expanding on the information obtained during the interviews, the students were asked to author a book with their parents as protagonists. For this activity they could use pictures or illustrations depicting the parent's life. Basic instructions were given during class, explaining the parts of a book and how to write it. As the students' work progressed, it was interesting to see how much they were learning from their parents and how meaningful the assignment was to them.

We decided to spend one week sharing the books. Some students had handwritten them, others had typed them, and a few had used a computer to design them, thus showing that "books can be simply three-hole punched and placed in a binder, or as elegant as computer-generated laminated pages bound together with a hard cover" (Ada, 1992, p. 49). All of them had found pictures of their families, and many had included postcards of their places of origin. The books were made in many shapes, such as the map or the flag of the country of origin, and others showed the seal or the national emblem.

Each day different students had an opportunity to present their biographies to the class. The student reading the book was assigned a special place in the center of the room and her or his presentation was recorded on a video. The students reacted positively: "Having to read our books in front of the class gave us a chance to share and to learn about the different cultures so we now understand each other better." The video was used during class for the students to see themselves in action, for the Parents' Open School Night, and to introduce the activity to children in other classes and different schools.

The collection of biographies was placed on display in the school's showcase and was also exhibited in the Media Center. The students used the books as texts and also decorated a bulletin board with them. The histories of all the families became a central part of our studies. Thus, the school began "recognizing the home, its richness and its very valid place in the curriculum within the context of critical pedagogy" (Ada, 1992, p. 46) and the children became authors of books having their parents as protagonists. As one high school junior remarked, "Writing biographies about our parents is symbolic of the fact that we are all authors and protagonists of our lives."

Voices Emerge

The final evaluation of the project included short essays written by the students in which they explained what the activity had meant to them:

> *This activity has brought me closer to my family. When you write about your background and share it with the class it gives you confidence and makes you learn about yourself. You learn to love yourself and be proud of your heritage.*
> *—HIGH SCHOOL JUNIOR*

> *To be an author at my age has helped me to get closer to my parents by providing a gateway for conversation allowing me to talk to them about subjects I could have never brought up otherwise, such as the struggles they had to go through to bring me into a free society.—HIGH SCHOOL SOPHOMORE*

A short form was sent home for the parents to share their comments about this activity with the rest of the students. Reading the parents' words was just as important, for it showed how grateful they were to be given an opportunity to take an active role in their children's education.

Conclusions: Reflection Leads to Action and Action Leads to Reflection

As the students and I reflected on what we had learned during the semester, we became aware of how the projects had impacted not only the lives of the students but also the lives of many others. In reaching out to my students and their families, I learned a great deal about their home-based experiences and their cultures.

Reflection led to action and our actions now lead us back to reflection. The question remained: What else could be done to encourage others to attempt a practical approach to critical literacy? I believe the answer is in our hands if we allow ourselves to open up to others in a continuous dialogue.

Questions for Reflection

1. What reflections do you have about your own teaching?

2. What signs are present that tell you your students are becoming critical learners?

3. How much of the time are you in front of the class?

References

Ada, A. F. (1992). *Parents and children as authors and protagonists: A critical pedagogy approach to home-school interaction* (pp. 46–50). Ontario, CA: California Association for Bilingual Education, Reclaiming Our Voices: Transforming Education for Cultural Democracy.

American Association of University Women. (1992). *Shortchanging girls, shortchanging America: A call to action.* Washington, DC: AAUW Initiative for Educational Equity.

Cornbleth, C., & Korth, W. (1980, Summer). Teacher perceptions and teacher-student interaction in integrated classrooms. *Journal of Experimental Education 48,* pp. 259–263.

Darder, A. (1991). *Culture and power in the classroom: A critical foundation for bicultural education.* New York: Bergin & Garvin.

Freire, P. (1970). *Pedagogy of the oppressed.* New York: Continuum Press.

Galeano, E. H. (1973). *Open veins of Latin America.* New York: Monthly Review Press.

Giroux, H. (1983). *Theory and resistance in education: A pedagogy for the opposition.* New York: Bergin & Garvey.

Good, T. L. (1987). Two decades of research on teacher expectations: Findings and future directions. *Journal of Teacher Education 35,* pp. 32–47.

Goodlad, J. (1984). *A place called school: Prospects for the future.* New York: McGraw-Hill.

Jackson, P. W. (1968). *Life in classrooms.* New York: Holt, Rinehart and Winston.

Ortiz, F. I. (1988). Hispanic-American children's experiences in classrooms: A comparison between Hispanic and non-Hispanic children. In L. Weis (Ed.), *Class, race, and gender in American education* (pp. 63–86). Albany: State University of New York Press.

Palmer, P. J. (1983). *To know as we are known: A spirituality of education.* San Francisco: Harper and Row.

Poplin, M. S. (1991). *A practical theory of teaching and learning: The view from inside the transformative classroom: Contributions of critical pedagogy.* Unpublished manuscript, Claremont Graduate School, Claremont, CA.

Ramirez, J. D. (1991). *Final report: Longitudinal study of structured English immersion strategy, early-exit and late-exit transitional bilingual education programs for language-minority children.* (Contract No. 300-87-0156). Washington, DC: U.S. Department of Education, Office of Bilingual Education.

Rosenthal, R., & Jacobson, L. (1968). *Pygmalion in the classroom.* New York: Holt, Rinehart and Winston.

Rubovits, P. C., & Maehr, M. L. (1973). Pygmalion black and white. *Journal of Personality and Social Psychology 24,* (2), 210–218.

Shor, I., & Freire, P. (1987). *A pedagogy for liberation: Dialogues on transforming education.* Westport, CT: Greenwood, Bergin-Garvey.

Silberman, C. E. (1970). *Crisis in the classroom: The remaking of American education.* New York: Vintage.

Sizer, T. (1984). *Horace's compromise: The dilemma of the American high school.* Boston: Houghton Mifflin.

Smey-Richman, B. (1989). *Teacher expectations and low-achieving students.* Philadelphia: Research for Better Schools.

4

Building a Research-Based Pedagogy to Enhance the Literacy of African American Students

FOLÁSADÉ OLÁDÉLÉ

For some time now, I have been doing research to gain support for pedagogical strategies that might enhance the literacy of African American students. I provide here a brief background for the discussion of pedagogy that will occur throughout this chapter, culminating in illustrations from my own practice over the years as a junior high school teacher in East Oakland, California, where I was fortunate to have been educated by my students, their parents, and my colleagues. In addition, over the past 10 years, I have read and been influenced by a number of African American scholars who are convinced that the "miseducation" of these students is related to the fact that the oppressor never wants to educate the oppressed (Delpit, 1988, 1995; DuBois, 1903/1973; Hale, 1986; Hilliard, 1991,

1995, 1997; Nobles, 1976; Woodson, 1934), and that, in fact, it is to the oppressor's advantage to keep the oppressed in darkness (Ani, 1994; Clarke, 1991; Wa T'hiongo, 1975). It might be said, then, that the failure of African American children to become literate and educated is by design; goes back to the conception of this country; is rooted in the European and European American world view and notions of "humanness"; is buttressed by the cruelty of chattel slavery; was extended by segregation; and is supported today by a vast research industry in the social sciences, education, and educational psychology (Ani, 1994; Baratz & Baratz, 1970; Douglass, 1845/ 1968; Hilliard, 1997; Jefferson, 1787/1982; Shujaa, 1994). In addition to this, many of these same scholars indicate that the control of images that White Americans have over Africans in America prohibits their ever seeing themselves in a positive light, and that one of the major places in which this control is manifested is in the schoolhouse (Gordon, Miller, & Rollock, 1994; Shujaa, 1994). As Carter G. Woodson wrote when discussing this issue almost 70 years ago (and, I might add, which is still relevant today):

No systematic effort toward change has been possible, for, taught the same economics, history, philosophy, literature and religion which have established the present code of morals, the Negro's mind has been brought under the control of his oppressor. The problem of holding the Negro down, therefore, is easily solved. When you control a man's thinking you do not have to worry about his actions. You do not have to tell him not to worry about his actions. You do not have to tell him not to stand here or go yonder. He will find his "proper place" and will stay in it. You do not need to send him to the back door; he will go without being told. In fact, if there is no back door, he will cut one for his special benefit. His education makes it necessary. (Woodson, 1934 / 1998)

The concern for the well-being of African American students has, however, not been limited to the realm of African American educators and scholars. Jonathan Kozol brought the problems of these students in the Boston public schools into bold relief in his book, *Death at an Early Age,* in which he decried the destruction of the minds and spirits of these youngsters (Kozol, 1967). He continues to write about these students and others in this country that make up a growing population of illiterates. In *Illiterate America* (1986), Kozol indicates that a solid one-third of all Americans are functionally illiterate and that another one-third possess minimal literacy competency. Kozol continues after 30 years to write about these distressing failures of the U.S. educational system. Quoting Eric Erikson at the outset of *Death at an Early Age,* Kozol writes:

> *Some day, maybe, there will exist a well-informed, well-considered, and yet fervent public conviction that the most deadly of all possible sins is the mutilation of a child's spirit; for such mutilation undercuts the life principle of trust, without which every human act, may it feel ever so good and seem ever so right, is prone to perversion by destructive forms of conscientiousness. (Erikson in Kozol, 1967)*

Although both Woodson's and Kozol's writing reflect seminal thinking that covers a period of almost 70 years, their thoughts have just as much meaning today. Very little has changed for African American students. Some believe that legislation meant to terminate segregation and to transform the education of African Americans has done neither. The *Brown* vs. *Board of Education* decision by the Supreme Court in 1954 has done little to improve the prospects for African American students who still suffer from "separate and unequal schools" (Foster, 1997; Hacker, 1991/1995). In fact, the situation in some ways has become worse, as indicated in a list of characteristics of the failure to achieve true equality in "integrated" schools framed by Hilliard in his essay "Forty Years after *Brown*" (1997). He outlines 15 outcomes related to the aftermath of the *Brown* decision, 8 of which are important to this discussion. They are as follows (Hilliard, 1997):

1. *Black Flight:* Blacks with financial and career options left their communities, leaving cities to decay.

2. *White Flight:* Whites took their businesses and tax dollars from cities or work in cities to suburbs, leaving cities to decay.
3. *School Closings:* Premier secondary schools in African American communities were closed as students were bused to integrate White schools.
4. *Fewer African American Teachers and Principals:* Ranks of African American teachers and principals were decimated. The percentage of African American teachers declined to less than half of what it was before "integration."
5. *Magnet Schools:* Magnet schools were created to attract an integrated population while African American schools received less attention.
6. *Increase in Educable Mentally Retarded Classifications:* The special education population skyrocketed, and continues to do so, almost in direct proportion to the success of "integration." The growth is especially pronounced in the "soft categories" of educable mentally retarded, learning disabled, attention deficit disorders, gifted, behavior disorders, and emotionally handicapped. African American children are resegregated in the desegregated schools because of disproportionate placements in these categories. This is so even where affluent and well-educated Africans Americans have integrated wealthy White suburbs!
7. *Discipline Problems:* Discipline became a key issue, as well as suspension, expulsion, and detention.
8. *Tracking:* Tracking has been used to resegregate schools by placing the African American population in the lower tracks.

In terms of literacy, specifically, other scholars have examined the manner in which the issue of language is used to inhibit the growth of African American students. Many teachers ignore the unique linguistic characteristics of African American students, putting them down when they speak, ridiculing them and overcorrecting them (Baugh, 1983; Delpit, 1995). This behavior may have contributed to resistance and rebellion in a number of African American students (Fordham & Ogbu, 1986).

Finally, scholars have observed that there are unique qualities and needs of African students in America that have never been accepted and analyzed by the Europeans who control the system of the delivery of instruction to this group of students (DuBois, 1903/1989; DeFrantz, 1995; Hale, 1986; Hilliard, 1995; Ladson-Billings, 1993).

As Lerome Bennett writes:

He who controls images controls minds, and he who controls minds has little or nothing to fear from bodies. This is the reason Black people are not educated or are miseducated in America. . . . The system could not exist if it did not multiply discrimination. It is no accident that there is a blackout on the Black man's contribution to American history. . . . An educator in a system of oppression is either a revolutionary or an oppressor. . . . The question of education for Black people in America is a question of life and death. It is a political question of power. (Bennett, 1986, p. 1)

Whether or not one agrees with Bennett's assertions, it is clear by now to the readers of this chapter that, in the minds of many African American scholars, African Americans have not been truly served by the current educational system, a system built primarily to meet the needs of White children. The reason for this is quite simple. African American children have their origins first and foremost in Africa. In this country, their beginnings were embedded in the enslavement process, which not only enslaved their bodies but their minds. Finally, African Americans have been educated in a continuously segregated environment where access to the quality of education available to Whites as well as access to an educational environment where mainstream American English is spoken has been denied.

In 1993, I wrote my first piece related to this subject in an article published in the *Harvard Educational Review,* "Giving Voice to the Voiceless" (Oládélé, a.k.a. McElroy-Johnson, 1993). At the time, I was grasping for straws. The inspiration for this article came out of my questioning some of the strategies being used by teachers who I admired in the Bay Area Writing Project (BAWP). Later, as a teacher in a junior high school in East Oakland, California, I began to document the necessity to tap into the ancestral heritage of my African American students in order to inspire them to become readers and writers. As I began to see their needs, I began to uncover my own need for transformation. I took on the study of the Yoruba culture and language and, as I did, an entirely different world, related to the discovery of who I am as an African person, opened to me. It was through my own enlightenment that I began to touch the spirit of my students and in doing so to transform myself.

Creating a Literacy Tapestry

There is an Akan symbol (see Figure 4.1) from the Twi people in Ghana depicting a bird that is at the same time looking backward

SANKOFA

FIGURE 4.1   Akan Symbol

and moving forward (Tedla, 1995). This symbol is fundamental to the creation of a pedagogy to develop critical literacy in African American students, for there will be no movement in these students until the past that they bring with them is addressed. This past extends from their ancestral beginnings in Africa as well as their forebears here on this continent to their current experiences at home and at school. The wisdom of Sankofa became apparent to me as I reflected on something one of my students wrote about how she saw herself as a reader and a writer. In a reflective essay describing what she had learned the past school year as a reader and writer, a student thanked me for the opportunities that had been created in the class. She reminded me that when she came to the class, she did not think of herself as a reader and writer and had never had to work as hard as she had in my class (reflecting on her past). At first, she admitted, she was angered by my insistence that she keep trying to do what she considered very difficult assignments, but after completing her assignments and reflecting on the work she had done, she felt gratitude for my confidence in her ability. She wrote this about herself:

> *This year [her past] I have forced myself to read more and more, to tackle books that I would have never tried to read before. I've done research and had to read a lot of things that I would have simply ignored in the past. I have read because I had to write these essays my teacher required us to write. At first I found the stuff we had to read really difficult, and I'd pretend that I couldn't do it, but my teacher wouldn't let me get away with that. She'd just put me with another student who was having an easier time, and we'd have to read together and write together. This stopped me from pretending that I couldn't do the work. I realized my teacher was serious about my learning. . . .*
>
> *As a writer [her present], I would describe myself as intelligent, realistic and respectful. As a writer, intelligence is very important. To write, you have to think. A person must show intelligence. Being real is all part of writing. If I am going to write, I am going to choose to write about myself. I want to*

*make the reader feel comfortable reading about my life and
me so they can visualize the things that I have gone through.
Respect is all in me. I respect myself as a writer, and I respect
you as a reader. As I look forward to high school [her future],
I feel confident as a reader and writer.*

It was through reading the work of my students and writing in
my own journals about my experience as a teacher that I began to
reflect more deeply on the foundation for my pedagogical strategies,
which was the process of my own literacy development. I became
aware that not only was it necessary for me to uncover and claim my
relationship to Africa, but that I needed to look at my most recent
past in my own childhood home in order to understand my own literacy development. I realized that this backward gaze was founda-
tional to my forward movement as a teacher and a mentor to my
students. I now know, in fact, that this type of reflection is a necessary ingredient for any teacher who hopes to be of assistance in the
literacy development of all students.

Everything my parents and grandparents taught me was sus-
tained by my elementary school. I attended Virginia Avenue School
in Louisville, Kentucky, across the street from our church. My principal, Mr. Lincoln, was my mother's principal. The walls of the
school were covered with beautiful black and white photographs of
famous African Americans—statesmen Ralph Bunche and Frederick Douglass; poets James Weldon Johnson, Paul Laurence Dunbar,
and Langston Hughes; educator Mary McCleod Bethune; libera-
tionists and abolitionists Sojourner Truth and Harriet Tubman;
and musicians Marion Anderson and Paul Robeson. On a daily
basis, Mr. Lincoln reminded us of who we are, where we came from,
where we could go, and what we could become.

Were parents, grandparents, and my principal aware of any pedagogical framework? No. They were doing something so endemic to
African people that it is rooted in our unconscious (Hilliard, 1995).
They were passing on the wisdom of our ancestors. They were building my education in the spirit of a power higher than themselves.
They were cultivating love of the creator, of ancestors, of parents, of
elders, and of self. They were embedding ritual, rhythm, music, rec-

itation, reciprocity, respect, and relationship into my psyche. They were teaching me the wholeness of life and all its relationships by weaving a tapestry of memory for me from the example of their lives. All of this has affected my practice as a teacher.

It is from this background that I set about building my own pedagogical strategies for developing the literacy of my students. Realizing that many students came to me with backgrounds different from my own, I didn't let that inhibit me. I decided that they were all my children, and my responsibility was as their caregiver. It was my duty to create the kind of learning environment of love and trust that would allow them to begin to feel the kind of bond with me that they might feel with any elder they respected.

Underlying Assumptions

My underlying assumption is that all students are teachable, and that the teacher/facilitator, as mentor, is very significant in the lives of growing children. This belief enabled me to create the environment, assemble the materials and methods, and establish the appropriate relationships so that teaching and learning could take place.

The learning environment is essential in addressing the literacy needs of African Americans. Like all youngsters, they cannot learn in chaos. In this instance, individual health and well-being play a significant role in both the teacher and the learner. I was rarely absent from class for illness or other personal reasons. Students could count on me to be there; they didn't have to worry about their teacher abandoning them. Our communication was polite, open, and sincere. Listening became very important for all of us. As a mentor, I had to get the students to work with me, and I could work with them. Those who came in with disruptive behavior understood that such behavior had to go. I decided that I was going to utilize the energy of the students for productive ends. We had to agree on the methods of effective communication. Specifics of that communication included:

- Show respect for the language that each student brings to class.
- One person speaks at a time.
- Listen when others are speaking.
- No laughing at others or making fun of them.
- No interrupting people when they're speaking.
- Speak clearly and loudly enough for other people to understand.

Beginning the Rebuilding Process

To get things done much more effectively, I used cooperative groups in my teaching, with the assumption that people in cooperation tend to produce more than those in isolation. I clearly emphasized that there is no *I* in *TEAM*.

Methods

During the first two weeks of the first grading period of the year, students showed little interest in class assignments, especially in listening, speaking, reading, and writing. They found it difficult to follow simple instructions, they could not quiet down easily to read material given to them, they could not speak to issues related to classwork and assignments but were constantly involved in personal discussions of social life and/or gossip, and they could not or would not write neatly and/or do any writing outside of purely scribbled pieces. They had little understanding of English grammar, formal structure (sentences, paragraphs), mechanics, punctuation, capitalization, or the writing process steps from prewriting to publication. They appeared to be belligerent and lazy, but my experience as an educator told me that the problem was one of fear about their ability to do what was required and a feeling of low self-esteem. Therefore, I attacked the problem on four fronts:

1. *The spiritual,* tapping into their humanity and connecting with their appreciation of their ancestors
2. *The affective,* building a positive attitude for learning

3. *The cognitive,* building the knowledge base so that the skills could be gained to meet the requirements of the curriculum
4. *The psychomotor,* building the type of environment of trust so that students could have reasonable freedom of movement

The Spiritual Connection

I began by tapping into the spiritual aspect of my students. This means that I understood their "humanness" and made it a priority to treat them with the care and understanding that all human beings require. I promoted the importance of culture and personal spiritual affirmation.

Greetings

I taught the students an African greeting in Yoruba, followed by one in Spanish, and I attempted the Hmei greeting as well. The point of the greetings was to show that all people have to be acknowledged and welcomed. The greetings expressed the need for human warmth in all cultures. Whenever a new student would come to the room, other students would teach him or her our greetings. If that student spoke a language that was new to us, that student would teach us a greeting in his or her language.

This attention to civility became the ground for our relationships. It engendered respect. Although this might seem fairly obvious, this practice was missing in my school environment. The decision to institute this practice was a crucial one and tended not only to improve my classroom climate but that of the entire school.

Recognition of Ancestors

After introducing students to the Yoruba greeting, which was interesting because of its newness to all of them, I spoke of the need to respect and honor our ancestors, families, nationalities, and cultures, and used this talk to illustrate that there were those to whom all of us were important. Students wrote down the name of an ancestor or someone they loved and who loved them and wished them the best. They did not share this information with anyone, but they were to remember who that person was whenever they had doubts about whether they were meeting the highest standards.

Affirmations

I taught the youngsters affirmations that they could use to help themselves cope with life and to build their self-esteem. Most of these affirmations were those that I created on the spot to fit appropriate needs. They were simple statements, such as: *I am able. I am intelligent. I am a good person. I am capable. I can succeed at whatever I set my mind to do.* I would have students think about these statements, sharing their thoughts with each other and/or writing their thoughts in a reflection journal. In addition, I used proverbs such as *"You must act as if it is impossible to fail"* (Ashanti proverb) and I used books of proverbs, such as *Wise Sayings for Boys and Girls* (Aromolaran, 1993). One day a student wrote me a note that read:

> *Dear Ms. Oládélé, I need some help from you. I need you to write me something to help me love myself. I see that you are one person who truly loves herself, and I need to love myself.*

I simply took a piece of paper and wrote, "I am a loving person, giving and receiving love. I love and I am loved." I gave it to her and asked her to look in the mirror each day and say it. Two years later I saw her at a competition where I was a judge. She ran up to me, full of joy and excitement, and reminded me that she was still using that affirmation.

Elders

I knew it was important to practice the African understanding of respect for elders. Many students had fallen into disrespect for elders because their trust had been betrayed. In addition, in African American culture, trust is earned. This is often very difficult for middle-classed White and Black teachers to comprehend; yet, it must be understood if any real literacy development is to take place (Delpit, 1995).

I set about building that trust by establishing high expectations for my students and myself—nothing but the highest—the best that we could do. That was our standard, and at the center of that was the understanding that they all had something to contribute. I believed they all could learn, and, because I believed this, I taught the students to believe in themselves.

I made myself available to my students. From the first day of classes, I met and greeted my students at the door of the classroom, and I stood at the door between classes, encouraging them to acknowledge my presence, greeting them as they came into the class, exchanging pleasantries with them, and expecting them to do the same with me. As odd as it seems, this was necessary, since many students had begun the school year pushing past me into the classroom without a word. I taught them to speak to me and to be courteous. I made myself available to help them at lunch time and after school. Students began to self-correct behaviors that were inappropriate when they saw me coming. They would say, "Man, don't you see Ms. Oládélé? You better respect your elder and yourself." One student reflected on her year in the classroom in this way: "Ms. O don't, I mean doesn't, let you get away with anything. She teaches you to respect yourself and to respect other people. Lots of kids aren't used to that because teachers just let them get away with anything, but not Ms. Oládélé, she will get you straight real fast."

Here, as I said earlier in this chapter, I practiced what I learned as a child. My mother taught me to respect my elders, and I communicated the significance of this teaching to my students.

The Affective Connection

Students must have a positive attitude for learning; a teacher can establish a basis for this by talking with students about the purpose of education and asking them to share their thoughts. From conversations with my students, I gleaned that each student had to be convinced that (1) they would be respected, listened to, and assisted in their work; (2) they could be successful in the academic environment; (3) they each had something to say and possessed experience

and skill, and they had prior knowledge that was valuable at whatever level they found themselves; (4) the environment would be safe
and predictable; and (5) the teacher/facilitator could be trusted to
be fair, interested in each student's achievement and true to his or
her word. In addition, students were assured that the assignments
given would be read and feedback would be given.

The Cognitive Connection

Listening

I focused on building the knowledge base to encourage development
in listening, speaking, reading, and writing. I began with the
requirement that students give their full attention to me when I
spoke and to each other when they were speaking. I made it a point
during the first few months of school to give short, five-minute talks
about materials we were studying, cultural pieces, and literary
pieces, and I required students to take notes so that they could write
a piece in their reflection journals about what they had learned. I
had them read these pieces to each other, take notes, and give feedback to each other about what they had heard. Each small group
had a recorder who took notes during small group discussions and
a reporter, someone who gave the reports to the large group. These
two responsibilities rotated through the entire small group. In addition, I used music with lyrics that they listened to and tried to
repeat. Listening to music is an excellent way of developing listening skills. I modeled good listening by being a good listener. I also
had them discuss the different levels of listening, from surface to in-
depth listening beyond the surface to the meaning behind the words
or sounds or the deep feeling that might be expressed there.

Speaking

I focused on the instruction of mainstream American English in the
classroom; however, I acknowledged the existence of the bilingual
nature of all of my students. Many African American students bring
a language from home to school that, for all intents and purposes, is
unique and very different from English. I taught my students to do
contrastive analysis between African American language and

mainstream American English. I did this through using daily oral language exercises as well as direct instruction on the phonological, morphological, and syntactical features of African American language as compared to mainstream American English. I showed them videotapes of individuals speaking both languages. They role-played situations in which they used both languages and discussed when it was appropriate to use either language. We discussed the issue of Ebonics, which became such a controversial subject in Oakland after the school board passed a resolution to deal effectively with the language education of Ebonics speakers. Students did research and clarified the facts/truth about Ebonics in relationship to what had appeared in the media. This not only served to clarify this issue but it also assisted students in developing critical thinking skills in relationship to what they hear in the media and elsewhere. They learned to research controversial issues.

I also dealt with Spanish in the same way, by pointing out the nature of acquiring English as a second or third language and the benefits of doing so. In order to give this type of instruction, I studied the work of a number of linguists and scholars (Baugh, 1983; Dandy, 1991; DeFrantz, 1995; Rickford, 1999; Smith, 1975; Smitherman, 1977, 2000; Williams, 1975).

In addition, I modeled mainstream American English in my own speech. I demonstrated the enunciation of words, the personal presence needed in a speaker in order to get the listener's attention, the appropriate modulation of the voice, and the eye contact needed when speaking to others. I provided opportunities for students to stand and talk to the entire class. They all spoke, taking turns. Although it was difficult at first, they became so confident that they actually began to support and encourage as well as correct each other. I recited poetry and I had my students memorize and recite poetry.

One student wrote about her English language development:

This year I have learned how to speak Main Stream American English, the differences between M.S.A.E. and Ebonics which means "Ebony Phonics," or "Black Sounds," and all other kinds of grammar that I was having trouble in. Since I have been in this class, I have improved as a student and as a person. Thanks to my teacher, I am now more open minded to the ways and customs of other cultures. She has inspired me to write more, to go with my feelings, and to always back my opinions up with facts. When I get in the tenth grade, I hope to learn how to write my own poetry, considering that now (after taking three writing classes this year) I enjoy writing.

Reading and Writing

Students were challenged to read books selected from the core curriculum. We all read for 15 minutes each day in every class. Students kept reading response journals for books that they read and for some selections taken from the texts. I also read aloud to my students every day. (See the section titled Literacy: Becoming Readers and Writers.)

I established the writing process as the way for students to write all of their assignments. That writing process consisted of five steps: prewriting, first draft or rough draft, revision, second draft, and final draft (proofreading and editing).

The Psychomotor Connection

Freedom of movement is important for all students who have a great deal of energy. I allowed that freedom of movement by establishing small groups in which students could work with each other. They could move around and talk to each other within the parameters of their assignments. In addition, books and materials were set up in one area of the classroom, and supplies were in another. In this way, the students could get what they needed. They were always free to approach me at my desk or as I walked around checking on their progress. In addition, I provided music for them and allowed them to hum or sway their bodies in rhythm to the music while they worked at their desks.

In essence, what I have been describing is the way I incorporated my knowledge from the past and the present with an eye on how to prepare my students for the future. One could say that I entered the classroom with my own bag of resources and my students entered with theirs. These bags contained the elements that were a part of the initial teacher/student interaction (see Figure 4.2).

Literacy: Becoming Readers and Writers

In order to become writers, students must be readers. The teacher creates opportunities for the use of reading materials in the classroom, tailored to the needs of students. Often in today's inner-city classrooms, teachers are confronted with students who never pick up a book to read on their own or go to the public libraries to read. Teachers must compete with the world of entertainment, video games, television, and music videos. In addition, many African American students have negative reading experiences initiated by their teachers. Teachers who ridicule and overcorrect African American students in the primary grades create students who are resentful, resistant, and full of self-doubt. Given all of this, it is necessary for the teacher to establish a great deal of trust. In addition, it will probably be necessary for the teacher to teach students the value of reading by being a reader and the value of writing by

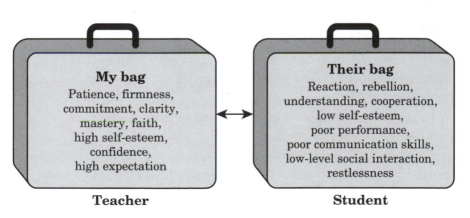

FIGURE 4.2   Tool Kits

being a writer. Teachers cannot compete with fast-paced commercial entertainment by simply assigning countless pages in textbooks and expecting students to read them and answer the questions that follow. Nor can teachers educate students entirely through the use of pop culture. Students have to be taught the purpose and value of reading and writing in relationship to their own lives. For students who have not gained basic literacy skills, there are excellent methods that can be applied in a very short amount of time to assist those who need help in such things as basic phonics and decoding.

Dorothy Strickland indicates in her work that students who have difficulty reading more challenging texts may be quite capable of understanding the content embedded in those texts. For that reason, teachers must be prepared to use a variety of techniques such as pairing the student with a proficient reader; oral reading, interpretation, and analysis; small group reading and analysis; and skills groups that are a part of the body of instruction—moving from whole to part in content and instruction. All students must always be included in the process so that readers who have difficulty are respected and not labeled as deficient. This practice is a part of African spirituality that recognizes the sovereignty of the human, the uniqueness of different human gifts, and the need to work cooperatively, not competitively, for the success of everyone.

The question is: What kinds of things are interesting enough to get youngsters who do not read to read? There are many packaged approaches, and one must weigh their effectiveness. I have applied an African cultural approach by using proverbs—short, pithy statements—to provide the beginning point for luring students into reading, thinking, and eventually writing. There are many excellent proverb books available. I used *Wise Sayings for Boys and Girls* (Aromolaran, 1993) which contained translations of authentic African proverbs as well as proverbs from other cultures. Proverbs appeal to young and old readers alike. As a result, many profound meaning-centered assignments and writing prompts may be derived from the higher-level thinking skills that proverb study promotes. By using this approach, a teacher can dovetail the reading of core works and grammar instruction with the proverbs to build meaningful writing projects for his or her students, while at the same time attending to the details of a curriculum that adheres to high levels of performance and rigorous standards of achievement.

Since reading and writing go hand in hand, I would like to discuss several writing prompts related to proverbs I chose from *Wise Sayings for Boys and Girls*. They were treated as a part of an overall thematic approach, dealing with the identity issues confronting young adolescents in middle and early high school years. Of course, these issues probably could be dealt with throughout life. For example, a year's instruction was constructed around several key identity issues, including friendship, self-reverence, wise decision making, and relationships with parents, neighborhood, and school. Using four proverbs as the foundation, students went on to extend their reading to core works, their writing to poetry and essays. The four proverbs are discussed next.

Choose your friends with the same care you choose your underwear.

This proverb was chosen initially because of a gang-related slaying of one of the students in my sixth-period English class. A week prior to the slaying, gang members from a nearby high school campus came onto our campus and burst into my room. They picked up a desk and threw it, pulled one of my students from his chair and began to beat him up, injuring him as well as those sitting next to him. The assaulted student was taken from the school, even though it was a case of mistaken identity. He was not the person the gang had been looking for. The perpetrators escaped, but their violence continued. The following week, they found their victim, gunning him down at a party. Shock waves of grief spread throughout the school the Monday morning following the tragedy. It became apparent to me that the students needed a constructive environment in which to express their grief and at the same time to accomplish their academic goals. I set about making my classroom that place.

They wrote obituaries and poetry as well as created beautiful illustrations, and, in so doing, began to develop deeper bonds with each other. One such poem is presented here:

The earth is like a flower; it always blooms.
The color represents the bodies of water,
the color of night, and the trees that breathe.
A flower is made up of all the colors of the rainbow
which represent us—black, white, brown, purple, or blue.
We're all one.
God made us all equal.
We, as people, should not spread hatred, would that be right?
For only hatred will lead to dark, dark nights.
A flower, a flower which is us, our bodies like petals so fair,
soft and sweet like a baby fast asleep.
A seed, which is our brain, that
can produce something very wonderful,
Instead of shame.
We must be kind to others like Martin Luther King,
teach strong sermons like Malcolm X,
and put this hatred that many people have to rest.

—L. M.

As a result of small group discussions, coming to grips with the deeper meaning of the proverb and relating it to the tragedy, students experienced growth through the writing they did about the tragedy, and accomplished the prewriting phase of their assignment. Now they had something to write about, and they began their first drafts, eventually working the proverb's theme through the revision and publication phases of the writing process. Many students expressed that they had never seriously thought about their friendships or considered them something to think about, but rather they thought friendship was something a person just fell into. Other students expressed concerns about being labeled snobbish, stuck-up, or "sedidy" if they didn't let "everybody be their friends." The death of this student in all of its tragedy provided a tragic opportunity to reflect on and write about the proverb and the issue of friendship. Through looking at friendship, students began to see that they needed some basis for making all of their decisions. So, we began our study of the following proverb:

A word is enough for the wise; it is for him or her to fill in the gap.

Building on our discoveries from the first proverb and the essays that followed, we continued our discussion about choices. It was apparent that friendship and selection of friends involve being willing and able to make wise choices, which require good self-esteem. But before understanding self-esteem, we had to give some time to the words *wise* and *foolish* so that students would understand the difference. One student wrote the following short essay:

One Word Is Enough for the Wise

The proverb explains that the wise people listen. They do what is being told to them, and they do what is expected of them. You only have to tell a wise person something once, and they'll do it. A foolish person will disobey and say okay, but never do it.

My brother was very foolish at one time. He would talk back to my mom and disobey her. My mom would tell him to do something, and he wouldn't listen. Now my brother is very wise. He listens, and he does what my mom tells him to do.

I have been wise because I have been doing what I have to do when I'm being told to, and I do what my mom expects of me. I've been foolish because in the past, I've disobeyed and done the opposite of what I was supposed to do.

I have learned that the wise will get somewhere because they get things done and the foolish will struggle the rest of their lives because they disobeyed, or they didn't do what they were asked to do. The wise will get somewhere, but the foolish will stay behind.

This discussion on wisdom led to the next proverb:

Self-reverence, self-respect, self-knowledge,
these three alone lead life to sovereign power.

After defining all of these terms, students began their group discussions on the meaning of the proverb, completed a worksheet, and were ready to write their essays. While students were working on these essays, each student chose a book from four titles that I had available that were written by African Americans dealing with concepts regarding the value of the self. In addition, they had to choose a book written by a Latin or Asian author. The titles included *Black Boy* by Richard Wright, *I Know Why the Caged Bird Sings* by Maya Angelou, and *The Autobiography of Malcolm X and Family* by J. California Cooper. The students read these books and kept a reading response journal.

In this journal, students wrote passages from the texts that interested them or about which they had further questions, and made their own observations about the writers. To conclude their reading and their thought process on self-reverence, students worked with the subject of racism and how it affects self-concept. These activities assisted students in their comprehension of the importance of having a sense of self-worth in a world that might attempt to destroy it. As a result of these activities, students began to affirm a growing sense of identity, as indicated in the following student's writing:

Self-reverence, self-respect, self-knowledge, these three alone lead life to sovereign power:

This statement is very true. If you love yourself, respect yourself, and know where you come from, then you are not controlled by others, and you are greater than all others, to the most important person in the world, yourself. I think life can become the most important thing to you while you're living, if you have all these things, and you won't be controlled by material things. It's like that song, "The Greatest Love of All," by Whitney Houston. It says the greatest love is learning to love yourself. In order to love others, you have to love yourself.

I mark Ms. Oládélé's words by saying "respect starts in the heart and mind." There was a strong point in those words. An example of respect in my heart is when people talk about me. I used to cry and I used to want to go home and stay there, but now I have learned respect for myself, so when I'm talked about now I feel sorry for those who are jealous of me. To me, I think it is very important for a young African American female to have respect.

Self-knowledge is harder for a young, black female, living in "downfall" America. In our school library, I don't find very many books on young, black females of today, so how are we supposed to find out where we, young black females, are? I am grateful to have a wonderful mother and sister, so when I have questions they're there, but what about those who are an only child and those without mothers. It is very important to have these things to be in control of yourself and your life.

I recommended this proverb to a friend who had been feeling low and down about herself because of an event in her life. She didn't understand it at first, but I explained it to her. After she understood it, she felt better. I'm glad I helped her out.

The fourth proverb is:

If you don't know who you are, you can hardly appreciate other people.

This led into our reading of our African American novels and biographies as well as works by authors from other cultures. To contextualize our conversations on the works mentioned earlier, we began with the poem "We Wear the Mask" by Paul Laurence Dunbar.

I used this poem to write a little talk in which I challenged students to follow my example by applying Dunbar's poem to my reflections on my own life. I read what I had written to them and gave them time to reflect and to write. One student responded with the following:

Reflection on "We Wear the Mask"

Being a young African American female that I am, I've already worn a mask to hide who I really am. When I was

younger, I remember trying to act like the rest of the girls, bad,
and thinking that I could do anything, but deep down inside
I felt funny acting like somebody I wasn't.

From elementary to where I am now, I have always hid-
den my feelings when something was wrong. When some-
thing was said or done to make me angry, I didn't say
anything. I just put it off as if nothing ever happened, and
when someone asked if I was okay, I lied and said yes when I
really wasn't.

The poem, "We Wear the Mask," in my opinion, is directed
to African Americans or "minorities." No matter how much
we are hurting, our mask smiles. When we are sad and when
we want to speak the truth our mask ends up lying, but for the
last few years, we have been changing slowly but surely. We
are speaking up for ourselves.

The only question that the poem, "We Wear the Mask," has
that I like is, "Why should the world be over-wise in counting
all our tears and sighs?" That is a very good question because
how would the world know about all the tears that we cried
unless they were us. Sometimes they (white people) think that
they know why we cried and sighed over the years, but they
don't know. I'm changing myself so that I won't have to wear
a mask, and I can show my true feelings.

Throughout the year, students wrote reflections about their
work and what they were learning. The following is one such reflection:

Writing this reflective essay has made me look back to
acknowledge what I have done and what I have learned this
past semester. I will tell you further about my work and my
thoughts as you read along.

First of all, I would like to say that I have learned a lot in
my English class. As I look back I'm very proud of all that I've
accomplished. I'm especially proud of my improvement on my
grammar. I think grammar was my main struggle, but now

that I understand more about it, my papers have less gram-matical mistakes.

I have to say that my most difficult assignment was the Reading Response Journal. It's because I didn't understand the assignment in the first place, and it was so long and kind of boring. Reading the book, Animal Farm, *was easy. In fact, I think I have read it so many times that I practically memorized the whole story, but keeping the journal was difficult and boring.*

Writing may not be my strongest point but reading is. I just love to read. I read all the time and read just about every-thing. It has something to do with the words and how it can take my imagination to a different time and place. So far, all the stories I have read were interesting. I love to read, but I hate writing. Another thing I'm not too good at is speaking. I think I can speak all right, but only when I speak to my friends or to individuals. Speaking to a group or to someone like my teacher is difficult.

This semester I wrote a fable, two short stories and two essays that I was proud of. I also read Animal Farm *by George Orwell and kept the reading response journal. I also learned about the differences between Mainstream American English and Ebonics, as well as about African history.*

These are some of my thoughts and examples of what I've done. I'm looking forward to learning more in the next semes-ter, especially on grammar. I still have trouble with it.

As stated throughout this chapter, recognizing the language, culture, and history of African Americans is essential to being able to develop their literacy and their academic achievement. Realizing the spiritual nature of the African American community is also vital. In order for a teacher to develop a more thorough understanding of the humanity of these students, that teacher must study and do the necessary research in order to build an effective pedagogy. Above all else, there must be an atmosphere of love, acceptance, and trust in the classroom.

Trust is one of the most important elements of teaching and being taught. Students must believe in themselves and trust their own abilities to learn and to be taught. They must trust the teacher/facilitator and be able to validate what they are being taught through their own experience. The teacher gains trust through his or her ability to create a learning environment in which she validates her own experience and that of the learner. Each student is teachable and is of value as a human being. The ability to create this environment is of the utmost importance because there are so many extenuating forces present in the community of learners.

Trust is inspired by the belief that every child, within reasonable parameters, given the gifts of human intelligence, and barring any unforeseen handicaps such as mental retardation or severe emotional problems, can learn everything that is being taught. Trust is accompanied by faith in the process of learning and being taught. It involves hard work on the part of the teacher/facilitator and learner in the maintenance of a positive environment. In this environment, everyone is free to be themselves within the context of respect for self and others. No one is ridiculed or harassed. Intimidation does not exist. To the degree that the teacher understands this and is able to implement it within herself or himself is the degree to which students will demonstrate it. Herein lies one of the major difficulties of teaching. The effective teacher is able to use his or her resource bag to create a transformation in the classroom environment so that the development of literacy can take place.

References

Ani, M. (aka Richards, D.). (1994). *Yurugu: An African-centered critique of European cultural thought and behavior.* Trenton, NJ: Africa World Press.

Aromolaran, A. (1993). *Wise sayings for boys and girls.* Berkeley, CA: Meroe.

Baratz, S. S., & Baratz, J. C. (1970, Winter). Early childhood intervention: The social science base of institutional racism. *Harvard Educational Review 40,* pp. 29–50.

Baugh, J. (1983). *Black street speech: Its history, struggle and survival.* Austin: University of Texas Press.

Bennett, L. (1986). The challenge of blackness. In J. Hale (Ed.), *Black children: Their roots, culture, and learning styles* (p. 1). Baltimore: Johns Hopkins University Press.

Clarke, J. H. (1991). *African world revolution: Africa at the crossroads.* Trenton, NJ: Africa World Press.

Dandy, E. (1991). *Black communications: Breaking down barriers.* Chicago: African American Images.

DeBose, C., Van Keulen, J., & Weddington, G. (1998). *Speech, language, learning and the African American child.* Boston: Allyn and Bacon.

DeFrantz, A. P. (1995). Coming to cultural and linguistic awakening: An African American educational vision. In J. Frederickson (Ed.), *Reclaiming our voices: Bilingual education, critical pedagogy and praxis.* Ontario, CA: California Association of Bilingual Education (CABE).

Delpit, L. (1988). The silenced dialogue. *Harvard Educational Review 58,* pp. 280–298.

Delpit, L. (1995). *Other people's children: Cultural conflict in the classroom.* New York: The New Press.

Diop, C. A. (1974). *The African origin of civilization.* Chicago: Lawrence Hill.

Diop, C. A. (1981). *Civilization or barbarism.* Chicago: Lawrence Hill.

Douglass, F. (1845/1968). In H. Baker (Ed.), *Narrative of the life of Frederick Douglass: An American slave.* New York: Signet, the Penguin Group.

DuBois, W. E. B. (1903/1989). *The souls of black folks.* Middlesex, England: Viking Penguin.

DuBois, W. E. B. (1996). *The education of black people.* New York: Monthly Review Press.

Fischer, C. S., et al. (1996). *Inequality by design.* Princeton, NJ: Princeton University Press.

Fordham, S., & Ogbu, J. (1986). *The Urban Review 18* (3), 176–206.

Foster, M. (1992, Autumn). Sociolinguistics and the African American community: Implications for literacy. *Theory into Practice 31* (4).

Foster, M. (1997). *Black teachers on teaching.* New York: W. W. Norton.

Gordon, E., Miller, F., & Rollock, E. (1990, April). Coping with communicentric bias in knowledge production in the social sciences. *Educational Researcher 19* (3), pp. 14–19.

Hacker, A. (1991/1995). *Two nations: Black and white, separate, hostile, unequal.* New York: Ballantine Books.

Hale, J. (1986). *Black children: Their roots, culture, and learning styles.* Baltimore: Johns Hopkins University Press.

Herrnstein, R. J., & Murray, C. (1994). *The bell curve: Intelligence and class structure in American life.* New York: The Free Press.

Hilliard, A. (1995). *The maroon within us.* Baltimore: Black Classic Press.

Hilliard, A. (1997). *SBA: The reawakening of the mind.* Gainesville, FL: Makare.

Jackson, J. G. (1974). *Introduction to African civilization.* Seacaucus, NJ: Citadel Press.

James, G. G. M. (1976). *Stolen legacy.* San Francisco: Julian Richardson.

Jefferson, T. (1787/1982). In W. Peden (Ed.), *Notes on Virginia.* Chapel Hill: University of North Carolina Press.

Jensen, A. R. (1968a). Patterns of mental ability and socioeconomic status. *Proceedings of the National Academy of Science 60,* pp. 130–137.

Jensen, A. R. (1968b). Social class, race and genetics: Implications for education. *American Education Research Journal 5,* pp. 1–42.

Jensen, A. R. (1980). *Bias in mental testing.* New York: The Free Press.

Kinchloe, J., et al. (1996). *Measured lies.* New York: St. Martin's Press.

Kozol, J. (1967). *Death at an early age.* Boston: Houghton Mifflin.

Kozol, J. (1986). *Illiterate America.* New York: Penguin Books.

Ladson-Billings, G. (1994). *The dreamkeepers: Successful teachers of African American children.* San Francisco: Jossey-Bass.

McElroy-Johnson, B. (aka Oládélé, F.) (1993, Spring). Giving voice to the voiceless. *Harvard Educational Review 63,* pp. 1, 85–104.

Nobles, W. (1976). Extended self: Rethinking the so-called Negro self-concept. *Journal of Black Psychology 2* pp. 15–24.

Nobles, W. (1985). *Africanity and the black family.* Oakland, CA: Black Family Institute.

Rickford, J. (1999). *African American vernacular English: Language in society.* (Oxford, England #26). New York: Blackwell.

Shujaa, M. (Ed.). (1994). *Too much schooling, too little education: A paradox of black life in white societies.* Trenton, NJ: Africa World Press.

Smith, E. (1975). Ebonics: A case study. In R. Williams (Ed.), *Ebonics: The true language of black folks* (pp. 76–85). St. Louis: Robert Williams & Associates.

Smitherman, G. (1977). *Talkin' and testifyin': The language of black America.* Boston: Houghton Mifflin.

Smitherman, G. (2000). *Talkin' that talk*. New York: Routledge.

Tedla, E. (1995). *Sankofa: African thought and education*. New York: Peter Lang.

Wa T'hiongo, N. (1975). *Decolonizing the mind*. Nairobi: EAEP.

Williams, R. (1975). *Ebonics: The true language of black people*. St. Louis: Robert Williams & Associates.

Woodson, C. G. (1934/1998). *The miseducation of the Negro*. Trenton, NJ: Africa World Press.

5

Words and Images That Provoke Informed Multicultural Identities

VALERIE ANDRIOLA BALDERAS

For some of my high school students, I knew that my classroom would be the last meaningful student-centered educational experience for my students, at least for some time. If this indeed were true, what understanding of the "system" could I pass on to them that might help them navigate more critically on the streets and in the workplace? I thought about which poet's words would bring them consolation and help them negotiate the meaning and purpose of their lives, whether they ended up in an institution or as successful citizens. —V. A. BALDERAS (1995)

Media content that promotes violence, sexism, and unequal power relations must be examined in the nation's classrooms in order to develop critical literacy that leads to true democratic participation and representation. Developing a critical conscious in media literacy can help people become sensitized to the inhumanity and psychological damage perpetrated upon those groups and individuals who are most negatively affected by absence of, misrepresentation, and misappropriation of culture.

Teachers concerned with these issues can help students interrogate cultural images within the context of their own lives by facilitating students' critical examination of media representation of "otherness." To this end, suggestions and examples of authentic cultural representation will be given that encourage students to develop a sense of empowerment through reappropriation of media representation that speaks to authenticity, social realism, and the beauty inherent in each ethnicity.

A constant barrage of violent and sexist images have desensitized the public's view of dominant and subordinate cultures. The need for a critical visual literacy allows students to become intelligent consumers in a mass-produced culture that fabricates dreams and desires.

Getting Started

A great place to begin a classroom examination of media representation is to bring in magazines and ask the students to do the same. The students may then create collages in order to critically examine media images. Through this pictoral representation, the students begin the process of turning visual art into words, watching for signs of representation or misrepresentation. For example, students may examine the strategies used to sell or influence the sale of certain products. They may investigate what those images say about the value of a man or a woman or what kind of man or woman is valuable. They may look at the role of the family or other strongly valued institutions. Stereotypes begin to emerge and the destructive or positive images are evident, leading to the formation of a strong bicultural or multicultural identity.

Students might also bring in ads that they object to and explain why, as well as ads that they feel are effective and that do not offend anyone. Classroom discussion will most certainly follow. Television programs, music, and movie clips might also be discussed in the same way and examined for their contributions to the conditions that create and maintain racism, sexism and, classism that promote societal conditions detrimental to all.

Our Walls Speak

Classroom walls are autobiographical in that they make statements about the teacher's beliefs, values, and multicultural awareness (or lack of) and suggest what is being transmitted to the students and communities. For example, what do walls say when they display commercialized images of Mexico only during Cinco de Mayo fiesta week? What do the walls say when they lack positive images? Why are Cesar Chavez, Martin Luther King, Jr., and other positive cultural images not displayed to instill pride, appreciation, and respect all year round?

Promotional items and media images depicting a straw-headed scarecrow with a sombrero, sarape, and mustache take their place on the walls during Halloween. Needless to say, these images cannot do much for the self-esteem of Mexican and Chicano students. Awareness of the stereotypes that sport a Mexican with a sombrero sleeping under a cactus or a chihuahua selling tacos can begin the open-ended dialogue between teachers and students. These images, brought into the classroom and interrogated, will begin the process of empowerment. Students will begin to question the types of mascots used at schools, the stereotypes in books and other media, as well as other symbols that serve to further marginalize various ethnic groups.

Resisting Passive Consumerism

By passively accepting these images, consumers support their pro-
liferation. Responsible teachers will help students recreate themselves with images and content that brings respect and a more
human curriculum into the school. In my classroom, I have a section
for the posters, pictures, and images that speak to what is most
important to me. Included are photos of my family and friends, pictures of artists I admire, and music I enjoy. Students and the rest of
the school community immediately know who I am and what I
value. In the curriculum choices I make, I instill pride in my students, while allowing for self-examination and critical analysis.
This is how I begin to build their trust. The physical environment
welcomes them. How do I begin knowing my students and letting
classroom visitors know them by reading the walls? At the beginning of each school year, my students illustrate a timeline and create self-portraits surrounded by positive statements they choose
that best describe them (e.g., "I am responsible," "I am cooperative,"
etc.). Other students and community members can immediately get
a sense of who these youngsters are and how they see themselves.
These words and images stay on the wall for the duration of the
course. As they produce words and images throughout the year,
these too are displayed on the walls. Our voices speak loud and clear
for all who wish to look, listen, and learn.

I am thrilled to see our walls come to life with large posters created by students as we complete units of study. For Black History
month in February, my students illustrated poems by various African American poets. For Hispanic Heritage month in September,
the students choose from a large collection of art books images that
speak positively and powerfully about who they are. I like to leave
the posters up long after the month is over. Lower primary students
are usually eager to illustrate but they tend to lose confidence in
that area over the years. It is rewarding to see that creative joy
restored, so I teach them how to trace, enlarging an image with a
transparency and the overhead projector. They then make the
image their own by painting, using colored pencils and markers, and
so on. Large images allow two to three people to work together on

one poster and will free up wall space so that everyone can be represented. People today read large images on movie screens or while zooming down highways, so why not recreate ourselves at least within the context of an environment we inhabit on a daily basis?

The Slave Auction: Reaction Leads to Action

Posters with degrading words and images, announcing what was later explained to me as a "fun tradition," were placed all around the high school. I was incensed and appalled and decided to use this experience to engage my students in a bit of critical analysis in terms of degradation and discrimination in their own lives. Our methods were discussion, interviews, and letter writing. My English-as-a-second-language (ESL) students and I first reviewed the history of enslavement in the United States and Mexico, and then discussed most students' countries of origin. Then, they were asked to respond in writing about the relationship between their personal experiences and this particular school tradition. I also shared my own written response, which was later read on the school news program and published in the school paper.

African American teachers, students, and administrators were interviewed to lend credibility to the offensiveness of this "tradition," which will hopefully be terminated next year. After the event, some of the more offensive posters were placed on my classroom wall, surrounded by my students' letters and topped with a picture of Martin Luther King, Jr. Not only did my current students gain awareness and understanding from this experience but new students and visitors could become immediately aware of what is and is not acceptable, at least in our classroom. A teacher has to choose which issues to address based on student needs and school climate and exactly how far each issue can be taken. This experience led me to reflect: Battles must be chosen and led carefully, because not all of them can be fought and won. Sometimes it may be necessary to remain silent and recharge for the more important issues that are certain to come.

Questioning Our Past and Recreating Our Future

Cruzando Fronteras / Border Crossings: A Student Play

What does a teacher do who is given an assignment to teach theater to recently arrived students who also need primary and English language development? Because this group of teenagers had limited primary language writing abilities, I decided to spend two days a week in a traditional classroom (with desks and chairs) for individual and group work. This provided a nice balance between what I felt the students needed and what they wanted—which was to be on stage.

The common theme of immigration emerged naturally as they began speaking and then writing about their life experiences in Mexico and their hopes and dreams for their new life in California. The leading questions they thought about were: Who am I and who am I becoming? Where have I been and where am I going? As the teacher, naturally I was the first one to answer these questions, as a role model, first by speaking and then writing. The students created their own list of questions, interviewed partners, and then presented their partners to the rest of the group. Each individual clarified his or her own reality by sharing the written version as a dramatized monologue.

Our classroom monologues helped build trust as well as empathy. The students' stories had strong sections that would lend themselves to dramatization, and so we collectively agreed on which sections we would be able to weave together into the story of just one family. The stories fell into three acts:

1. Economic Reality and School Life in Mexico
2. The Journey and Border Crossing
3. The 10-Year Aftermath

We felt it was important to jump 10 years to address the social reality of so many immigrants not only in our community but in other communities as well. In our particular story, two of the children achieved the "American Dream" and two fell victim to drugs, gang life, and teenage pregnancy.

The production was to be produced in the fall semester, but given the constraints of a group that had never produced a live theater production nor witnessed one, the work was proudly presented in March of the spring semester. The extra time allowed the main characters to attend a bilingual play in a nearby city and to work with professional actors in workshops and sound recordings. These sound recordings were an important part of the production, because not enough written material could be developed. For those working on productions, a word of advice: At some point, you have to stop writing and start staging! Thus, visuals, in the form of slides, became the fill that also translated the essence of the story for monolingual English-speaking audiences. Also, costumes, props, and scenery were kept to an absolute minimum. Students are very good at filling in the story line and scenery.

Speak, Write, Action

An effective teacher always wears several hats and pulls from each in terms of personal past experiences and abilities and attempts to share these with his or her students. My part in this production, aside from organizing and directing, was chief editor. At some point, after the student input was exhausted, I stepped in to edit and type up a final script from which to begin dramatizing their work. Some of the dialogue, although powerful, did not work well with the story but found its voice in the narrative monologues that accompanied the slides. Those were two very powerful moments in the preproduction process: to see one's thread woven into a new story and to hear one's voice professionally recorded and woven in with other spoken voices and sound effects that filled the auditorium as well as our hearts.

Ideally, the slides depicting community images, both positive and negative, would have come directly from the students—given time and money for cameras, film, and processing—or would have been produced by a photography department, which, in our case, was not yet in place. A collaborative effort here could have created further opportunities for language and social development among diverse student groups. Instead, in the interest of time and money, I used slides I had from other past productions and shot new images from the community. The teacher oftentimes gets to learn more than his or her students; I was frustrated that my students were left out of this potentially powerful community learning opportunity.

After the performance, so many people from the audience came up to the students to thank them personally and cried because this story was also their untold story. I was grateful to those fellow teachers who were willing to take their students to the day performances. It was tough convincing some of them to "trust the visuals" to transcend the language barriers. I reminded them of the popularity of opera productions that communicate stories in foreign languages. Many letters were received from "mainstream" students that were also touched by a reality of which they had not previously been aware.

Given more time, we would have worked toward a bilingual production. We were a brand new high school and I felt it was important to set precedence in the area of fine arts that reflected our student population. So we pushed hard for a first-year multimedia production with first-year drama students, and we succeeded quite well. The students earned a two-page spread in the yearbook. I know their lives were changed for the better, forever! They soon became the bilingual leaders of the school, speaking and performing for various parent and community events.

The Family History Writing Project

The first time I saw family histories was in Sacramento, California, using a program called Hyperstudio, which connected with special effects photos, drawings, visual text, and voice-over. These multimedia, multicultural stories were then transferred to video so that each child could take home a copy. I was eager to learn more about my Southeast Asian students, but very little information was available in the libraries of the community. The Hyperstudio family stories were a powerful entry into this new community and validated a lived history not found in the standard curriculum textbooks.

This presentation by a wonderful Chinese teacher gave me a new-found passion for future student projects that later led to my dissertation study on lived history as part of the school curriculum. As a high school teacher with several groups of students, I opted for a simpler version, using photos and/or drawings and text that was word processed and bound in a photo album or spiral binding with cardstock covers. These family masterpieces were read aloud to other classes and community groups and appreciated by all.

Each time I have facilitated this writing project, the results and circumstances have been different. And, like any project, the process becomes cleaner with practice. There are a few guidelines I would recommend:

- Allow more time than what you foresee, because the highlight of this project is the sharing of the books with as many audiences as possible. They will begin their writing from the notes and information they have gathered from family members. I provide my students with a list of questions to guide their dialogues and they usually add to it.
- Students' notes will become paragraphs that will be edited by the individual and his or her peers, first on paper and then on the computer screen. The use of Author's Circle at any time during the writing process will assist the author with his or her editing and revisions. It is important to give the students a list of guiding questions early in the school year or semester as a homework assignment to do with their parents.
- Most of the parent involvement will be in the form of interviews the students will conduct to collect their information. Many

cathartic moments from these home interviews have been reported back to me and ultimately are revealed in the quality and content of the students' writing. Some questions for reflection that will emerge from these exchanges will focus on how the students would want their lives to be different from that of their parents and grandparents or even brothers and sisters. They may want to include this new knowledge in their writing about their future goals and dreams. (See Chapter 3 for a step-by-step process.)

- The most transformative opportunity offered from the interview/dialogue portion is that these intergenerational exchanges contain the possibility of creating new knowledge that can be powerful in the students' development of a strong bicultural identity.

- Often books become rushed at the end of a semester. If there is no spell-checker available with your computer(s), the editing process can go on forever. I have had to explain to audiences that ours is a work in progress. Have the students start drawing or collecting photos even before the writing begins. Sometimes students will have to send away for their photos. Some of these will be of poor quality or will need to be enlarged and/or touched up. Many will want to have them copied in color or black and white in order not to use the originals.

Some of the photos brought in by the students may lend themselves to dialogue on culture, class, sexism, and other topics as the two or more worlds are examined across multi-generations. Both photos and text should inspire critical dialogue. Some of the drawings and/or text will be so beautiful that you may wish to copy the entire book to inspire future groups and to make contributions of local history and folklore to your library. Specific themes that emerge can be extrapolated to create new books, such as *Our Immigration Stories* or *Our Grandmothers* or *Our Parents Lives as Farmworkers,* and so on. These collections can be used to enter into future units of study with other students reading aloud those selections that focus on a common theme.

We kept a simple format of one photo or drawing and one paragraph per page. (For early primary students, I recommend one to three sentences per page.) I try to encourage most of the writing before the page layouts begin so that the photos do not become the prime motivators of the text. They will, most likely, inspire additional writing. The writing process is important to achieve the best results, so a file needs to be set up for each student. Continuous student and teacher feedback through conferencing and Author's Circles greatly enhance the quality of the final product.

Since each book will be different, I encourage the students to include poetry and writing from previous studies and writers' workshops. These additions will give the book a more autobiographical touch as well as aid the student in his or her own personal growth. The students should realize that they are working on a very special project with a subject matter that deserves respect and care. This project will teach them new skills and valuable information about their community for critical examination as well as cultural appreciation. The students' books will become gifts they give themselves and their families and an important addition to the school or classroom library. And finally, the book format should be kept simple and according to age-group abilities. This project is recommended for upper primary through high school (and even adult school).

For lower primary-age students, coauthoring and parent involvement is a must! If the students are not familiar with keyboarding, it might not be wise to two-finger type too many paragraphs. However, the on-screen peer-editing moments are powerful learning opportunities, so word processing is definitely well worth the time spent. The books are also more reader friendly and professional looking when typed with attractive fonts. Every extra touch and effort the teacher facilitates (within his or her time and materials budget) will instill pride and a sense of accomplishment in the students. The teacher should also be sure to have copies made and bound of exemplary samples to inspire future writers and fellow colleagues.

A Teacher Gathers Community Images/Information

Your Light, Flower and Song: *A Book of Healing*

For students to examine and recreate themselves through images and text, teachers need to serve as models and engage in the writing process. I photographed the chronology of a funeral involving a double homicide of a brother and young sister, allegedly gang related. This local tragedy that devastated our community was close to our hearts, especially since the same family had been hit with another tragic death just two years prior. My first intention was to bring the photographs back to the classroom for discussion, writing, and healing purposes. While sitting in church observing the rituals, the singing and chanting, which became the text, rang forth like a mantra lifting our spirits and easing the pain. Because the words and images do not seek to sensationalize senseless violence, the possibility exists to open up critical dialogue and raise student consciousness about existing conditions of oppression and the choices people make and the outcomes they create in response to those conditions.

Any book with strong language and/or images that interrogates the social realities of marginalized people can be a powerful tool for reflection and constructive action. These books lend themselves to some powerful personal examination and reflection. They also often inspire letters demanding preventive situations for young people that will be conducive to constructive outcomes, such as after-school art centers. Herein lies an opportunity to treat a harsh social reality with sensitivity, thus transforming communities with proactive behavior that empowers its members rather than victimizes them into fatalistic retreat. The book, filled with photographs, reads as follows:

Tu Luz, Flor y Canto/Your Light, Flower and Song

Cuando se troncha una flor,
La gente enciende muchas
velas.
>Las encendemos.
>Las encendemos.

When a flower is taken, we light
candles.
Los niños plantan un arbol.
>Lo plantamos.
>Lo plantamos.

We plant a tree.
Al arbol le cuelgan valentines.

Se los colgamos.
Se los colgamos.
On the tree, we hang up
Valentines.
En los valentines escribimos
mensajes.
>Se los escribimos.
>Se los escribimos.

and write messages on them.
En el altar le ponemos fotos.
>Le ponemos fotos.
>Le ponemos fotos.

Photo from Valerie Balderas's book, *Your Light, Flower and Song*

We place pictures on the altar.
Las voces del coro nos levantan
el espíritu.

> Levantamos el espíritu.
> Levantamos el espíritu.

The voices of the choir raise our
spirits.
El padre los rocía con incienso.

> Los rocía.
> Los rocía.

The priest showers them with
incense.
Le lloramos mucho.

> Pobrecita angelita.
> Pobrecita angelita.

We all cry for the little angel.
La mama pierde lo que mas
quiere.

> La mama pierde.
> La mama pierde.

A mother loses what she loves
most.
Los amigos pierden a un
hermano.

> Los amigos pierden.
> Los amigos pierden.

Friends lose a brother.
La maestra pierde a una niña.

> La maestra pierde.
> La maestra pierde.

A teacher loses a little girl.
El director pierde a un
estudiante excelente.

> El director pierde.
> El director pierde.

A principal loses an excellent
student.

Los vecinos se organizan.

> Nos organizamos.
> Nos organizamos.

The neighborhood takes action.
Los padres nos guían en una
procesión.

> Nos guían.
> Nos guían.

The priests lead us in a
procession.
Suben el ataud al carro.

> Lo subimos.
> Lo subimos.

A coffin is placed in the hearse.
Los seguimos al panteón.

> Los seguimos.
> Los seguimos.

We follow them to the cemetery.
El papa les da su última
bendición.

> Los bendice.
> Los bendice.

A father gives his last blessing.
La gente observa en silencio.

> Observamos.
> Observamos.

Everyone observes in silence.
La gente se despide echando
flores.

> Echamos flores.
> Echamos flores.

We say good-bye with flowers.
Los recordamos con flores.

> Los recordamos.
> Los recordamos.

We remember them with flowers.

Donde hay mariachis les
cántaremos dulces canciones.
 Les cántaremos.
 Les cántaremos.
With mariachis we'll sing sweet
songs for you.
Para el dia de tu quinceanera te
bailaremos un vals.
 Te bailaremos.
 Te bailaremos.
For your quinceanera, we'll
waltz for you.
En el dia de tu graduación
soñaremos los mismos
sueños...

Te los soñaremos.
Te los soñaremos.
On your graduation day, we'll
dream the same dreams for
you...
de un mundo mejor porque
seremos tu luz, flor y canto.
 Seremos luz, flor y canto.
 Seremos luz, flor y canto.
of a better world as your light,
flower and song.

References

Ada, A. F. (1996). The Pajaro Valley experience. In A. F. A. I. Campoy (Ed.), *Language and transformative education: Readings.* San Francisco: University of San Francisco Press.

Balderas, V. A. (1995). To be alive in struggle: One teacher's journey. In J. Frederickson (Ed.), *Reclaiming our voices.* Ontario, CA: California Association for Bilingual Educators.

Balderas, V. A. (1998). *Tu luz, flor y canto / Your light, flower and song.* San Jose, CA: Nautilus Publications.

Cummins, J. (1995). Knowledge, power, and identity in teaching English as a second language. In F. Genesee (Ed.), *Educating second language children: The whole child, the whole curriculum, the whole community* (3rd ed.). Cambridge: Cambridge University Press.

Freire, P. (1973). *Education for critical consciousness.* New York: Seabury.

Freire, P. (1993). *Pedogogy of the oppressed* (3rd ed.). (Myra Bergman Ramos, Trans.). New York: Continnum Publishing.

Giroux, H., & Purpel, D. (Eds.). (1983). *The hidden curriculum and moral education: Deception or discovery?* Berkeley, CA: McCutchan Publishing.

hooks, b. (1994). *Teaching to transgress: Education as the practice of freedom*. New York: Routledge.

McLaren, P. (1998). *Life in schools: An introduction to critical pedagogy in the foundations of education* (3rd ed.). New York: Addison Wesley Longman.

6

Critical Literacy and Visual Art
A Living Experience

JULIA MARSHALL

*Art constitutes one of the rare locations
where acts of transcendence can take place and
have a wide-ranging transformative impact.*
—BELL HOOKS (1995)

Making art can be a powerful tool for developing critical thinking and literacy. In approaching art in education, educators often focus on the aesthetic and technical aspects: art production skills and the refinement of sensibilities that art making can engender. The potential of art practice for stimulating awareness of social, cultural, racial, and class issues and for developing critical judgment about these issues is neglected. The primary objectives of these exercises are to encourage and enable students to pinpoint issues and ideas that are important to them and to explore them in depth, to invite students to think critically for themselves, and to bring imagination and personal interpretation to that process.

Critical Literacy and Art Practice

What Is Art Practice?

I have adopted the term *art practice* to describe an evolving learning experience that employs observation and critical thinking in the process of creating images. In art practice, art making is not an isolated event done for purely aesthetic reasons or recreation; rather, it plays a pivotal role in the emergence and construction of knowledge. In art practice, what is observed or what has been experienced is transformed into images. Through those images, new information is created and truths are revealed that lead to new knowledge, further exploration, and deeper understanding. Reflection and critical thinking are essential to that process and integrated with art making all along the way.

The methodology of art practice is similar to the educative process outlined by Paulo Freire in his seminal book, *Pedagogy of the Oppressed* (1970). In developing a format for coming to critical consciousness, Freire mapped out a spiral path of reflection and action through which critical consciousness emerges. This map serves as a model for art practice, as art making is considered a form of action.

Art Practice: Generating and Developing Critical Literacy

> *Using the arts as a way to teach subject matter places the learner in the position of truly working with ideas and taking control of learning in a manner that is at once intellectual, personal, meaningful and powerful.*
>
> —*MERRYL GOLDBERG (1997)*

The dynamic fusion of thinking and action that art practice encompasses is the key to developing critical literacy though art. Art practice offers ways of processing information personally and collectively that involve critical thinking, questioning, problem posing, and working through solutions creatively. In the process, the artist gathers information and shapes it into a form that tells the artist more about the information than he or she knew before the making.

This process goes beyond recording and expression to constructing and learning. In short, art practice represents a way of teaching oneself. The power of art practice lies in two essential elements of art making: the engagement of imagination and the transformation of information into images.

Imagination

> *Consciousness always has an imaginative phase, and imagination, more than any other capacity, breaks through the "inertia of habit."—MAXINE GREENE (1995)*

Bringing imagination to critical thinking about issues allows the process to transcend the mere gathering of information and analysis of the implications of that information. Although the harvesting of information and reflection on its meaning are the springboard for art practice, they are just the beginning. Engaging the imagination brings to the process personal interpretation and attribution of meaning and the infusion of hope (Greene, 1995). It also opens up the process to the exploration of issues and ideas through play and experimentation. The artist becomes personally engaged and acquires a sense of personal agency. In a collaboration, this feeling of empowerment is amplified by a sense of solidarity. In imaginative critical art practice, there is a message, subtle or overt, that the world can be changed through creative thinking and problem solving.

Image Making

> *These symbol systems—these codes of meaning—are the vehicles through which thought takes place. . . . Through the use of symbols the human mind, can create, revise transform, and recreate wholly fresh products, systems and even worlds of meaning.—HOWARD GARDNER (1982)*

Art constitutes a symbol system or language, and as a language it is a vehicle for communication and expression. In considering visual images, people most often think in terms of their capacity to communicate information. Therefore, visual literacy is commonly thought of solely as understanding the cultural and communicative role of images. But as a language, visual images also shape and generate thought. It follows that visual literacy should also include understanding how the mind creates visual images and how this production is an active process of learning and creating.

Creating visual images begins with the mental process of visualization, taking thoughts or information and translating or imagining it in visual terms. What people see around them gives them models and inspiration in their creation of images, but information that is not visual can also be the subject or inspiration for visual images that are made.

The second step in image making is manifesting the mental image in a material object or picture. The process of translation of the mental into the physical image (art making) is crucial, for it creates further meaning.

How is image making an educational process? Taking information and distilling it into visual representation is an act of making connections between information and concentrating it into an image or metaphor. This metaphorical process creates new meaning and fresh insight. As metaphor, the image can be subtle, complex, and multilayered, and it can reveal hidden information. In this way, the act of visualizing and image making is an act of creation, of making new informative connections, and of learning from that creation. It is construction of knew knowledge. Creating images is at the core of art making and, as a learning process, is a vehicle for understanding one's world. Visual literacy is an important part of critical literacy, and art practice is an effective way of developing it. Consider the following examples:

- In observing and reflecting on images around them, students acquire skills in deciphering and understanding those images. These images can be pictures and icons from advertising and popular culture as well as art forms.
- In actively making their own images, students develop personal insight into how images are generated and what they can mean.

- In deep reflection on images and image making, students can come to understand the intersection between personal and cultural image generation. It is through the actual making of images that they get a personal experience with them, coming to understand personal and cultural origins and meanings of visual signs and symbols.

How Does Art Practice Work?

Five primary components of art practice can evolve in this sequence: idea generation, research, reflection, art making, and further reflection. The process need not always be in this order and can include repetition of any part of the process as necessary. At times, research comes first; sometimes making art can be a form of research, which catalyzes further research and art making. For example, some ideas can be generated from personal experiences:

1. Teachers can begin with developing ideas and themes for the art work through group brainstorming and cluster mapping of students' ideas.
2. Students can select topics to research.
3. Sketching and recording of ideas follows leads into the making of the art images.

In this form of art teaching, the techniques and materials are secondary to the concept explored; they are in service to the concept and therefore are chosen after the idea is developed and for their appropriateness to the subject.

Reflection on the Art Project

In an ideal situation, reflection prepares the way to more art making, which incorporates images and ideas culled from the information and experience of the initial art project. This continuum makes the art experiences deeper, richer, and more meaningful.

In focusing on the acquisition of critical literacy in art practice, one must always ask: What am I learning? What do I know now that

I didn't know before? This takes the emphasis away from the formal qualities, craftsmanship, and preciousness of the product and puts it firmly in the realm of process and the learning that occurs in it.

Students Making Sense of the World

Art practice that focuses on important issues that affect students will help them make sense of the world they encounter. It will bring about awareness of what they already know and will introduce them to new information. Most of all, the learning that occurs will be personally meaningful, because the student has been engaged on an emotional and subjective level.

Codifications

Looking at, interpreting, and thinking about art works or visual images are common practices in conventional art classes. In the art practice suggested here, observing and reflecting on images and art are also very important to the projects, but the intent and content are different. The focus is not on formal and expressive qualities of an art work but on the message it conveys. The art or images viewed are presented as catalysts for thought and discussion. Here, the visual material presented becomes a *codification*.

The codification is an invention of Paulo Freire (1973), who developed and used codification to generate thinking and to develop critical consciousness. A *codification* is an image that depicts a social, political, or cultural condition. For Freire, a codification was an illustration that he showed to groups of people who could not read. In the illustrations, people would recognize their own reality and in discussion of the image, they came to critical consciousness of that reality.

In the art projects presented here, the codifications have the same objective but their form is different. Our codifications take two forms: works by artists or cultural images from the environment presented for reflection or inspiration to the students before or during the lessons, and the art work produced by the students themselves. In the first case, images presented as codifications are often contemporary art work that focuses on social, political, or cultural issues. In the second case, the art work created by the students catalyzes reflection on students' realities and attitudes, leading to critical consciousness.

The Projects

The following projects conform to Freire's (1973) notion of problem-posing education—that is, art projects that call for critical thinking, imaginative problem solving, and open-ended solutions.

Project One

Writing Our Own Histories:
The History Book Project

> *I didn't know I knew so much about social studies books. I didn't pay much attention to them. I just looked at them because the teacher told me to open them and read them. I didn't think I was reading them very much. I didn't realize that I knew about them until we made our own book. When we did, I really thought about what those books are about and I realized how much I knew.*
> —*EIGHTH-GRADER, POTRERO HILL MIDDLE SCHOOL*

History presents a prologue to current events and its narrative shapes the way people think of themselves and their stories. Often presented in textbooks as truth, histories are, in reality, interpretations of events. Students need to understand that the history they are reading in these texts is filtered through the lens of the writer and presented from his or her personal and cultural vantagepoint.

Critical Literacy Objectives

- Students work in groups to rewrite history books. They alter existing, out-of-date textbooks by cutting, collaging, drawing, and inserting their stories into the books.

- Students learn about history textbooks by closely examining the components of the books.
- Students compare their conception of history to that of the textbook.
- Students research the historical events and people who have contributed or shaped their cultural and ethnic heritages.
- Students examine their lives and their backgrounds in the context of historical text.
- Students see themselves as historical figures who have the capacity to build the future.

Art Objectives

- Students employ collage techniques using found images.
- Students manipulate existing images by adding their own images.
- Students tell stories and convey ideas though visual images, such as maps and time lines.

Other Objectives

- Students examine the past and imaginatively interpret it by writing their own autobiographical stories.
- Students learn to work together.
- Students learn from each other about their respective lives and legacies.
- Students find common ground among themselves.

Codifications—The Project

- Illustrated history books, political cartoons, and other items
- Collages of Romare Bearden, story quilts of Faith Ringold

Materials

- Old history books or textbooks, preferably books about American history with lots of pictures
- Photographs or photocopied photographs of students

- Collage materials: images from magazines, construction and drawing paper, scissors, pencils, pens, watercolors and brushes, glue sticks, and so on

Art-Making Procedure

1. *Begin by brainstorming.* Discuss the nature of history books and historical writing, asking questions such as: What is truth? What is interpretation? How do people's histories differ? What is our (your) history? How does our (your) history fit into (or not fit into) the one recounted in the books? How do we write our own history?
2. *Take photographs of students.* Photos of students' heads and shoulders will be more successful. Color copy the photographs so students have many pictures to use.
3. *Divide students into groups of four or five.* Each group chooses an old book that they would like to manipulate. This book should be recyclable.
4. *Students examine the books.* The students will look at the text and images, and brainstorm how they can use and alter them.
5. *Students interview their parents and relatives about their lives and heritage.* Students research their heritage in the library.
6. *Students write stories of their past, present and future.*
7. *Students develop time lines and maps.*
8. *Students insert their stories into the books.* Pictures, maps, images, and time lines already existing in the books' backgrounds become part of the books.
9. *Each group collages and paints the cover of the book.*

Reflection

1. Students display and discuss the books and the stories and images in them.
2. They discuss their role as historical figures and make speculations about the history books of the future that will recount their lives and present-day events and conditions.
3. Students discuss how they can make history.

Project Two

Portraits of Social Activists/Leaders:
Gigantic Puppets

> *Making the puppets was fun. I made Mohatma Gandhi. I read about him in some books and I got a picture of him and then I made his face and his body. He was a really great man and I got to learn what he did and then I got to make him.*
> —EIGHTH-GRADER, JAMES DENMAN MIDDLE SCHOOL

An activist or social leader often embodies a cause, a value, a concept, or a time in history. Exploring this person's life, thoughts, and actions brings a human face and reality to ideas and conditions that otherwise can seem abstract and impersonal. In researching a social leader, students can find common ground with the person examined and come to understand that person's motivations, convictions, and time in history. They can also discover the complexities of human thought and behavior behind sweeping historical or ideological movements and concepts.

Above all, social leaders offer positive personality traits and provide examples of moral consciousness and heroic action. A leader's story can inspire students to emulate his or her thoughts and actions and to imagine how they also could shape the future.

Why make portraits? In making an artwork, an artist develops a detailed knowledge of every aspect of the work. In making a portrait of a leader, the artist/student develops a double intimacy: one with the work and an imaginary one with the person portrayed. An imaginative bond is developed through the student's authorship of the portrait; he or she comes to know the subject in a close way by personally interpreting the image of the subject.

Overview

In this project, each student researches an activist and makes a gigantic puppet of that person. Along with making puppets, students will do the reflection activities listed at the end of the lesson plan.

Materials

- For *faces,* chalk pastels, 2' × 3' pieces of corrugated cardboard, posterboard, newspaper, masking tape, wheat paste, tempera paint, and brushes
- For *bodies,* chalk pastels, 18" × 24" construction paper, glue, and collage materials (such as yarn, felt, buttons, colored paper)
- 8' pieces of lath

Critical Literacy Objectives

- Students learn about social, cultural, and political issues and conditions today or in historical eras.
- Students acquire research skills. They will study the lives of people who are/were making change, paying attention to personality characteristics such as empathy, compassion, strength, and perseverance.
- Students come to understand how one's personal life intersects with one's public life.
- Students examine their own convictions and imagine how they could follow their convictions and affect public life.
- Students acquire a sense of history—that is, that history is shaped by people and that the future is being created today.

Art Objectives

- Students observe and depict the human face and body in the form of a caricature.
- They learn about facial characteristics and facial expressions and how they convey personality.
- Students learn construction techniques for papier mache.
- Students use mix media collage techniques and paint.

Codifications

- Photographs of activist leaders (e.g., Martin Luther King, Jr., Malcolm X, Aung Sung Su Kyi, Rosa Parks, Nelson Mandela, Albert Schwitzer, Cesar Chavez, Mahatma Gandhi, Susan B. Anthony)

- Gigantic puppets by Wise Fool Theater and Bread and Puppet Theater, two groups that produce and perform plays that address social issues

Art-Making Procedure

1. *Begin by brainstorming.* Ask the students if they know any social leaders. Give them examples to get the process moving.
2. *Each student selects an activist that she would like to research and portray.*
3. *Show pictures of activists.*
4. *Students do research on their subjects.* The *World Book Encyclopedia* is an excellent resource for finding biographies and photographs.

Faces

To make a large relief sculpture of a face:

1. Sketch the face of the subject using a photograph for reference.
2. Draw an oval on a piece of 2' × 3' piece of corrugated cardboard, and cut it out using a utility knife. (The teacher can do the cutting if necessary.)
3. Tape and staple (using staple gun) the oval to two pieces of lath that cross each other. The horizontal piece must be as long as the face is wide. The vertical piece will hold the body form and will also act as the handle of the puppet. It should be 8' long.
4. Make facial features by using posterboard and crumpled newspaper. Tape the features in the proper places on the front surface of the cardboard oval. Tape them on *well.*
5. Cover the entire oval, features and all, with one layer of newspaper strips that have been dipped in wheat paste. Then cover the face with one layer of brown paper towel dipped in wheat paste. Allow to dry.
6. Paint the faces using tempera paint.
7. Glue on collage materials such as yarn or torn paper to make hair.

Bodies

To make a small, flat body:

1. Fold an 18" × 24" piece of construction paper in half lengthwise.
2. Fold the paper in half cross-wise. Fold the paper in half again.
3. Open up the folded paper and draw a stick figure following these guidelines: The head extends from the top edge of the paper to the first fold. The shoulders are on the first fold. The waist is on the second fold. The knees are on the third fold. The feet are on the bottom edge of the paper (see Figure 6.1)
4. Draw around the stick figure to give flesh to the bone structure you have created in the stick figure.
5. Cut the figure out.
6. Attach collage materials to the figure to make clothes: colored paper, images from magazines, ribbons, cloth, buttons, or whatever you like.

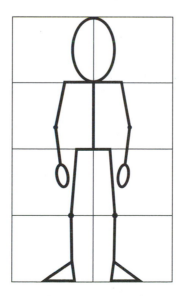

FIGURE 6.1 Model/Diagram for Bodies of Puppets

7. Attach the body to the handle of the puppet. Slide the oval head of the paper body under the large papier mache face (or cut it off).

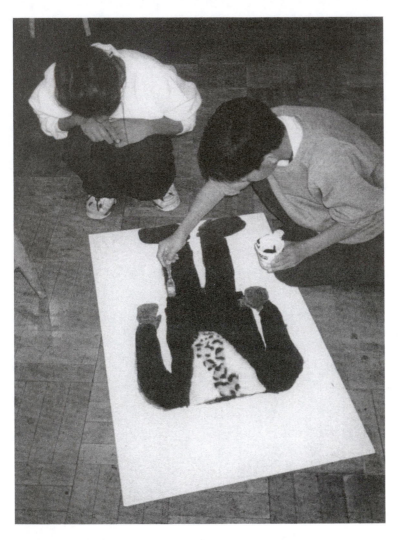

Painting the Puppet Bodies, James Denman Middle School, Seventh Grade

Reflection

1. Students write stories about the pivotal events in their subjects' lives.
2. Students write plays about their subjects. The plays can be written by groups of students and can involve interaction and dialogue between the subjects. Students will perform the plays.
3. Each student will conduct an interview with his or her subject. In the interview, the student can touch on their subject's primary ideas, motivations, actions, and historical context. This will give the student the opportunity to write in his or her subject's "voice."
4. Students will keep workbooks, sketchbooks, or journals in which they store:
   Photocopies of photographs of their subject
   Drawings of major events from the subject's life

Puppets of Social Activists/Leaders, James Denman Middle School, Seventh Grade

Information they have gathered from their research

Preliminary sketches for the puppets

Their own reflections on the subject

Their own observations on social, cultural, and political conditions

Their own solutions to problems

Their own dreams and wishes for the future

Conclusion

These projects are especially designed for middle school students. The goal is to catalyze discussion and to promote visual and critical literacy. Beyond these goals, the projects offer students an opportunity to play, think imaginatively, and personally interpret critical issues and ideas. Let us not forget that making art can be very satisfying and enjoyable as well as challenging. The personal and emotional benefits of play and creation that art making involves bring joy and a sense of personal accomplishment to the learning experience in very concrete ways. Teaching and learning toward critical literacy is very serious work but it can be done in ways that are active, imaginative, and deeply engaging.

Questions for Reflection

1. How do you integrate history and art in your curriculum?
2. What opportunities do your students have to explore their ancestral roots and see themselves in the history of this country?
3. How comfortable are you in bringing up topics that may be controversial and not part of the history books the students read?
4. What resources do you have available to further your knowledge on some of the feats and defeats people experienced coming to this country?

References

Cahan, Susan, & Kocur, Zoya. (Eds.). (1996). *Contemporary art and multicultural education.* New York: Routledge.

Freire, Paulo. (1970). *Pedagogy of the oppressed.* New York: Continuum.

Gardner, Howard. (1982). *Art, mind and brain.* New York: Basic Books.

Goldberg, Merryl. (1997). *Arts and learning: An integrated approach to teaching and learning in multicultural and multilingual settings.* New York: Addison-Wesley, Longman.

Greene, Maxine. (1995). *Releasing the imagination: Essays on education, the arts and social change.* San Francisco: Jossey-Bass.

hooks, bell. (1995). *Art on my mind, visual politics.* New York: The New Press.

Lacy, Suzanne. (Ed.). (1995). *Cultural pilgimages and metaphoric journeys, mapping the terrain, new genre public art.* Seattle: Bay Press.

Langer, Suzanne K. (1970). *Philosophy in a new key: A study in the symbolism of reason, rite and art.* Cambridge, MA: Harvard University Press.

Lowenfeld, Viktor, & Brittain, Lambert W. (1987). *Creative and mental growth.* New York: Macmillan.

Neperud, Ronald. (Ed.). (1995). *Transitions in art education: A search for meaning, context, content and community in art education, beyond postmodernism.* New York: Teachers College Press.

Stuhr, Patricia. (1985). Multicultural art education and social reconstruction. *Studies in Art Education, National Art Education Association 35* (3), 171–178.

Stuhr, Patricia, Petrovich-Mwanki, Lois, & Wasson, Robin. (1992, January). Curriculum guidelines for the multicultural classroom. *Art Education 16* (2).

7

Teaching Critical Writing to Secondary Students
Speaking Our Worlds

ASPASIA NEOPHYTOS-RICHARDSON

*The most exciting thing we can remember is going into the classroom and having...
deep and powerful dialogues [where] we also shared and examined our own lives.... As students we were taking control of our lives, getting to know ourselves, and we were able to share our feelings with others. If we had known that sharing and looking closely at our cultures, our lives, and society was so transforming, we would have done it sooner!*
—STUDENT AT CHANNEL ISLANDS
HIGH SCHOOL (OXNARD, CA)

Secondary teachers, seeking to engage students' enthusiastic participation in their own learning, must ask themselves how they can:

1. "Pose knowledge as a critical problem relevant to students' lives" (Olsen & Mullen, 1990).
2. "Lead students to see curriculum as something they co-develop for themselves" (Olsen & Mullen, 1990).
3. Establish trust and interactive goals.
4. Ignite in students the sense of excitement, of possibilities, of vistas and new worlds which diversity has to offer.

Getting students to participate in learning challenges the traditional experience of education as something *done to* students. Rather, transformative teaching embraces students as cocreators of the context in which learning occurs.

Most students, however, do not possess the skills needed to cooperate actively in cultural democracy in the classroom or society. They have not exercised critical thinking enough, nor spent much time reflecting on the meaning of their experience in school. It is important for educators who live and work in societies of students who vary by ethnicity, language background, and socioeconomic status to choose what and how to teach in classrooms while honoring both diversity and excellence.

This chapter provides a model of creative-critical writing that bring teachers and students to a reflective level of understanding of their personal lives in relation to the world. They have as their goal the fostering of critical thinking and coming to "voice" as the basis for excellence in academic achievement. These models, like all creative processes, can be adapted to any age level across all disciplines, languages, and cultures. Interspersed in the narration are excerpts from teachers', students', and parents' reflections about their experiences with these models.

As an assistant professor in the School of Education of Chapman University, I am involved in the preparation of teachers in cross-cultural communicative competence. I begin by asking my students to relate what they are learning to their own personal experiences. As they reflect on and tell their stories in class, these teachers experience a transformation. They feel empowered and hopeful about the task of reaching students' minds and hearts and become interested in hearing the stories of others. They understand that, to achieve their goal of creating a harmonious and participatory learning environment, they are faced with the same obligations as their students. That is, they have (1) to become reflective about their own cultural responses in the classroom and beyond and (2) through the transformative process of self-understanding, to develop empathy regarding the cultural contexts affecting the thinking and behavior of their students. In other words, teachers must become conscious of the prejudgments that order their lives based on their cultural traditions and past experiences (Ricoeur, 1992). Once teachers acknowledge the powerful influence that culture and past experience have on their present thoughts and actions, they simultaneously clarify the relationship between their own lives and those of their students.

> *My father was born into a very poor farming family. Through hard work, self-determination, and a good education, he was able to rise above poverty. I assumed since poor people of past generations, including my father, had risen above poverty, so could people of today. Yet, it is true that poor people of today do not have the chances that the poor of yesterday had. Often this brings about a feeling of hopelessness and a "why try" attitude. I realized what I had been doing: placing poor children as if they had gone through life with my, or my father's experiences, and not theirs.*
>
> *—SECONDARY TEACHER, WEST CONTRA COSTA UNIFIED SCHOOL DISTRICT*

Bellah and colleagues (1985) write that what is needed from history is not merely information about the past, but some idea of how one has gotten from the past to the present. People need to understand how their lives are woven into the fabric of the world and what role they can play in improving life for themselves and their community. In traditional education, the teacher possesses the knowledge and passes it on to students. In this model, teachers are sometimes students and students are sometimes teachers. Teachers' life narratives become the basis for their own empowerment as they reflect on and appropriate their past actions (Ricoeur, 1992).

It's an ongoing lesson for me to understand that when people feel pain or fear from racism their feelings are real. Whether or not their feelings are appropriate or a correct response to the reality is not for me to say and not within my reality to make a judgment.
                    —*SECONDARY TEACHER, SAN FRANCISCO*
                              UNIFIED SCHOOL DISTRICT

Central to the meaning of this kind of teaching is James Banks's Approaches to Multicultural Curriculum Reform (Banks & McGee-Banks, 1989) and Alma Flor Ada's (1997) Language and Transformative Education. I first encountered Banks at a time when I realized that teachers in my classes were having difficulty moving beyond the superficial manifestations of culture (song, dance, cuisine, etc.). Teachers were timid about contacting cultural informants, preferring instead to keep to the safety of library research. At that time, I found that introducing Banks's four approaches helped teachers see how they could create a curriculum that incorporates the voices of all members of the learning community. Banks's framework is introduced in Figure 7.1 as four interdependent levels. Whereas in traditional schooling, the *Contributions* and *Additive* levels are addressed, here the greatest stress is placed on the *Transformation* and the *Social Action* levels. With Banks, teachers found effective and mutually supportive ways to connect the classroom with the community and gained confidence in moving into true multicultural teaching and learning.

The model of teaching and learning presented here is focused on bringing readers to a deeper self-understanding through the transformative power of text. The Creative Reading/Writing Process, adapted from the innovative work of Alma Flor Ada (1997), is very effective, as evidenced in the teachers' reflections interspersed throughout the next section. They examine the condition of their own democratic and caring process within the context of school and community. Each person's voice and life narrative become important to the growth process in the context of the classroom.

FIGURE 7.1   Approaches to Multicultural Curriculum

Level 1. Contributions Approach	Level 2. Additive Approach
Classroom activites focus on the heroes, holidays, and other discrete cultural elements such as: • Food • Artifacts • Clothing • Holidays • Maps • Heroes • Music, art, dance • Posters • Geography • Climate	Provides for content, concepts, themes, and perspectives to be added to the curriculum without changing its structure, such as: • History of the culture • History and current circumstances of the immigrants • Precepts guiding the culture • Use of literature of the culture to provide depth of understanding • Bibliographies • Useful websites
Level 3. Transformation Approach Changes the structure of the curriculum to enable students to view concepts, issues, events, and themes from diverse ethnic and cultural perspectives. Learners seek out individuals of other cultures (cultural informants) to enhance their learning. The voices of all members of the community are heard, and issues relevant to the community are discussed. The curriculum seeks to include the multiple perspectives of and new understandings gained by students. The outcome is the appreciation of and respect for one's own and other cultures.	**Level 4. Social Action Approach** Students make decisions about important social issues and take actions to help solve them. Authentic, generative problem themes are agreed on and a problem-posing methodology is used. Curriculum is co-constructed through reflection and dialogue, where the role of the teacher is colearner, listener, and facilitator, not conveyor of knowledge. Heightened awareness developed in class enables students to take action and intervene to right social ills suffered by members of the community.

Source: Adapted from Banks and McGee-Banks (1989).

The Creative Reading/Writing Process

This article made a statement that I completely agree with: "Collaborating with parents requires that we confront our own fears of difference and open our classrooms to discussions of topics that may raise tensions among the values of different individuals, groups, and institutions." Children learn by modeling others' behaviors. If influential adults in their lives do not attempt to understand other cultures, how can I expect that child to seek his / her own understanding of other cultures? I cannot. I must become their model that steps outside my comfort zone.—SECONDARY TEACHER

The reading process is a dialogue between the reader and the written word. Reading and writing define each other and therefore cannot be separated—hence the term *reading / writing*. It is the process by which the reader becomes exposed to the indivisible connection between the world within and that outside. At one and the same time, students' imaginations are exposed to possible new worlds to be found in the text while their personal passions and dreams are brought to the surface of their consciousness by what they read. There is a mutuality of inward and outward flow that occurs and is at the heart of learning. Instead of the traditional approach of seeing literacy as the decoding of symbols and the accumulation of vocabulary words and their meanings, literacy here becomes the door to experimentation and ultimately to self-knowledge. Students read and reflect on text in order to get at their own perspectives and feelings.

This is the very first time that I have read an article on the four ethnic groups. Before, I never got a chance to understand their cultures. I am Chinese and I have many Asian and Caucasian friends but I do not have any Native American friends. I have several African American neighbors but I do not understand them a lot. Most of my previous knowledge of the other cultures was basically from my friends' experiences and feelings, and that may be fragmented....Before I tell my students to appreciate other cultures, I have to appreciate them first.

—ASIAN SECONDARY TEACHER, MT. DIABLO UNIFIED SCHOOL DISTRICT

Generally, once students become proficient in this form of interactive reading/writing, they appear to welcome the opportunity to be reflective about themselves, their work in the classroom, and their lives in the community. For example, in the classes that I teach, the classroom becomes an oasis of safety and community where the group welcomes "differences of opinion" with interest and even pride. There is a sense of "possibility" and openness to each other that this form of teaching encourages. Students help each other work out problems, they bring in materials to share, and they appear to enjoy doing assignments. Through the process of interactive reflection, students and teachers become co-developers of the learning experience, listening with open hearts and minds to fellow students. As mutual respect grows, and they begin to share their dreams and fears, pains and pleasures, students develop an enhanced sense of personal emancipation and a deeper understanding of the fundamental interconnectedness of all human existence.

To become empowered, students must be heard and affirmed frequently. They must also challenge aspects of their own voice that disempower or oppress other people.

I try to encourage students to help one another to practice cooperation and also utilize individual strengths. Yet, what honestly needs to occur is a change within myself.... My classroom at times seems an entity of its own. I need to examine my own values and interests so that I can begin to develop a stronger balance between my personal individuality and my communal responsibility in a way that extends and actually helps to connect all of the different components of my life.

—SECONDARY TEACHER, CONTRA COSTA UNIFIED SCHOOL DISTRICT

Theoretical Framework

The framework for the Creative Reading/Writing Process is presented graphically in Figure 7.2 as four interdependent quadrants. This is done to emphasize the four-in-one integrity of the response required. For this process to be effective, the writer must include all four phases when reflecting. It is important that the teacher become familiar with these phases in order to guide students toward addressing them.

In formulating the framework, Alma Flor Ada (1997) helped bring to light the way in which critical literacy occurs. It essentially clarifies four distinct phases of reading/writing:

1. *Descriptive Phase:* Readers attempt briefly to record the facts (events, emotions, thoughts, and objects) that are described in the text.
2. *Personal Interpretive Phase:* Readers reflect on feelings and memories that may be evoked in this encounter with the text. This connects them with their own past.
3. *Critical Phase:* Readers evaluate the arguments put forth in the text to the best of their present judgment.
4. *Creative Phase:* Readers have a future orientation, applying their new-found knowledge gained as a result of this encounter with the text. Thus, the text becomes a bridge from the past into a possible future. Incidentally, *text* in this case can mean literature, film, theater, and visual depictions.

Objectives

Objectives for the Creative Reading/Writing Process include:

- To establish trust and confidence
- To foster students' and teacher's self-understanding
- To guide students to the realization of the power of the text
- To move students toward multicultural literacy
- To help students to continue developing fluency and proficiency in English and their primary language

FIGURE 7.2   Creative Reading/Writing Phases

Descriptive Phase	Personal Interpretive Phase

• Transmits information given in the text.
• Corresponds to the initial phase of comprehension. Though both useful and necessary, it is by no means the sum total of reading.
• Answers the questions:
  a. Who?
  b. What?
  c. Where?
  d. When?
  e. Why?
  f. How?
 	
(this is a brief synthesis of the most important concepts and facts presented)
	• Weighs the information against the reader's experiences, feelings, and emotions.
	• Brings the content within the reader's grasp, thus making the process relevent.
	• Helps the student understand that true learning takes place only when new information is analyzed in the light of one's previous experience.
	• Ensures that each reader's individuality is an integral part of the learning process.
	• Validates the reader's life and experiences, recognizes his or her culture.
	• Answers the questions:
	  a. *Do you know of (have you seen, felt) something like this?*
	  b. *Have you ever done (thought about, wanted) something similar?*
	  c. *What would you (your family, friends) have done (said)?*
	  d. *How did you feel after reading this? Did you like it? Did it worry you? Frighten you? Make you happy?*
	
	(corresponds to the past)

Critical Phase
 	
• Invites reflection and critical analysis in terms of reader's experience, knowledge, past readings.
• Helps reader draw inferences about the information presented.
• Answers the questions:
  a. *Could this have turned out differently? What are some alternatives? What do they depend on? What would they lead to?*
  b. *Are there other writers who have discussed the same issues? Who benefits (suffers) from this decision? Is it fair?*
 	
(corresponds to the present)
	Creative Phase
	
	• Completes the reading process by making a connection between reading and each reader's world.
	• Encourages each reader to make decisions for bettering and enriching his or her own life by applying the new knowledge acquired (decision made).
	• Answers the questions:
	  a. *How might you . . .*
	  b. *How could you avoid . . . ?*
	
	(corresponds to the future)

Source: Adapted from Ada (1997).

Activity Guidelines

The guidelines for the Creative Reading/Writing Process help the teacher plan successful experiences for students. Teacher voices have been incorporated where necessary to demonstrate the development of creative reading/writing:

1. It is important that the text chosen for students has relevance to their lives. As I am dealing with teachers in multicultural classrooms, the texts I choose include the work of Sonia Nieto, Gloria Ladson-Billings, Cristina Igoa, and Laurie Olsen and colleagues. Teachers find these to be extremely pertinent to their situations.

2. The framework (Figure 7.2) is given and carefully explained to students. Then I suggest that students take a blank sheet of paper and fold it in four, labeling each quadrant to match the framework. This is used for note-taking during reading or viewing.

3. Students individually read/interact with the text (book, play, film, or video). They jot down notes in the appropriate quadrant as ideas and feelings arise in response to the reading and include the page number of the part of the text to which they are responding.

4. Students then read and interpret their notes and prepare a written reflective response in the form of a four-paragraph essay organized into the four phases of critical reading/writing. Most students tend to write each phase in a separate paragraph, as can be seen in the following examples:

(Descriptive Phase) *The film,* Color of Fear, *portrays the frustration and pain of racism in the United States. Eight North American men of African, Chinese, Japanese, Mexican, and European descent present their histories and experience of racism. Most of the film yields the fight and struggle of living together and the invisible racism in this country, yet the end of the film promises hope for the future.*
—STUDENT TEACHER, CHAPMAN UNIVERSITY

(Personal Phase) *I first saw the video* Color of Fear *as a sophomore in college, and it erupted so many feelings inside of me. I just remember crying and crying because it brought up many memories from the past. Memories of having to defend my own race, my people, . . . memories of the shame I felt because of things that have happened to people of African descent. Also the shame I felt for blaming people for the situations they were in.*
—STUDENT TEACHER, ST. MARY'S COLLEGE

Others organize their paragraphs to include several phases simultaneously. Here, I read through carefully and identify each phase to make sure all are represented in the text. Here is an example of phases sharing a paragraph:

(Critical/Creative Phase) *I believe that a reteaching of the potential good everyone has to contribute needs to occur. At this point in time, individuality is emphasized as a personal commodity for one's marketability and future success in society. It is not addressed as a donation, an important addition to the well-being of the whole....I try to encourage a sense of responsibility to the class as a whole. We discuss our conflicts openly and problem-solve together.*
—*SECONDARY TEACHER, MT. DIABLO UNIFIED SCHOOL DISTRICT*

5. The quality of thinking is stressed rather than the quantity of written words. A rule of thumb is two handwritten or double-spaced typewritten pages per completed reflection. For people who like to write more, the maximum could be two single-spaced pages. I like to limit the writing because (a) it requires students to consider carefully what they will say and (b) I read and respond interactively to each reflection. Students are encouraged to choose only one or two aspects of the reading to respond to, particularly those that elicit strong responses from them. In this writing process, students learn to simplify and synthesize, as can be seen in this example:

(Descriptive Phase) *Cristina Igoa's chapter from* The Inner World of the Immigrant Child *requests teachers to under-*

*stand the true inner feelings, thoughts, fears, depression, con-
fusion, isolation, loneliness, exhaustion and mixed emotions
of immigrant children so that they may overcome their culture shock and either assimilate or acculturate into the mainstream culture. It is construed that with the help of a
supportive teacher, such immigrant children may embrace
their own culture and the American culture.*
        —STUDENT TEACHER, CHAPMAN UNIVERSITY

6. Depending on the teacher and the resources available, writing
   can be done either in English or a student's home language, and
   can be written by the student or dictated to someone who is literate and proficient in the language.

7. The teacher responds interactively to students when reading
   their reflections by sharing personal experiences or observations, as well as offering technical suggestions and advice
   focused on improving the student's writing abilities. My personal responses are not prescriptive but reveal my thinking at
   the moment. Students, without exception, express particular
   appreciation for this type of communication. I find that their
   writing expresses more profound concepts and at the same time
   becomes more elegant and moving as they become engaged in
   our dialogue. Here is an example of an interaction:

*Often, I have heard that we lose some of our childhood spon-
taneity as we approach adulthood. In the past I have attrib-
uted this to the fact that we are expected to accept
responsibility for our lives, a very serious undertaking. As an
educator I have often heard teachers and administrators
complain about students who are struggling as being "imma-
ture" as if this were some evil. I really liked Dewey's concept
that immaturity simply means that one has the capacity for
growth. When you look at a struggling student as one who
has so much to learn, you see [him or her] in a more positive
light.*
        *—ADMINISTRATIVE INTERN, SAN RAMON
        UNIFIED SCHOOL DISTRICT*

8. Students feel more prepared and able to participate in a rich classroom conversation transformed by the clarification and strength of their convictions. This reflective dialogue noticeably engages all members of the group, and not just the few vocal students that tend to dominate in the traditional classroom.

Notes to the Teacher

At first, students may need guidance with reflective reading because they may not be culturally experienced with one or more of the phases. Some, having never connected school learning to the events in their personal lives, may find it difficult. Many may be reluctant to share personal experiences with others unless the level of trust in the classroom is high. Others may never have gone beyond regurgitation of the basic parts of a text. This type of exercise requires the selection of materials that interest students and challenge their assumptions.

Based on an evaluation of each student's written reflections, the teacher will have to address the technical aspect of writing either with individual students or the whole group. Here, it is important that the teacher know and work with the strengths and weaknesses of each student in the group and use language arts and second language acquisition methodologies to guide students in improving their writing.

As examples, I sometimes pair up a student who is having trouble understanding the text with another who has a compatible personality and mentoring skills. Or I might use a Venn diagram on the board to help students organize their thoughts about different aspects of the text. Perhaps I will model style by doing a class brainstorm session and then writing up their responses in the appropriate form. Sometimes I work individually with students, giving them specific suggestions to help them improve their writing skills.

The teacher's personal expression is a powerful and effective way to establish trust and confidence in the classroom because the teacher is taking risks along with the students. As a result of the mutual vulnerability, students often share their most important experiences and insights. The reward of this transformative model of teaching and learning is the highly developed sense of mutual caring that is manifested among the members of the group.

Variations

Separate but Equal

This is a good way for the group to become practiced in the four different phases of reading and to realize the importance of using all four in reflection. After explaining them and having the students practice using the phases individually, I divide the class into groups of four. Each group becomes responsible for one of the four phases. I give the whole class the same text to read, and then each group reflects on the text from their specific perspective (Descriptive, Personal, Interpretive, Critical, and Creative). Finally, each group makes a brief presentation to the class. This requires each group to come to consensus about what it thinks is important to say.

Group Literacy

This is an excellent way to have students read and reflect on a book together. After starting out skeptically, students very quickly become seriously involved in their group discussions and their individual reflections because of the benefit they perceive in being able to discuss their ideas together. In this powerful model, each student hears her or his individual "voice" while remaining at the heart of the group. Here, the teacher remains the facilitator.

1. Students are formed into groups of four or five in which they will stay while reading a book together. Using community building activities such as those described in Tribes (Gibbs, 1995), the group builds a strong common bond; the group even chooses a group name and logo.
2. The Descriptive Phase for each new chapter is done by students individually, possibly as homework. Each student reads the chapter and takes notes of her or his understanding of the basic points made as well as any questions that come up during the reading. Generally, the teacher need not read these notes.
3. In their groups, students together share their notes and questions and help each other come to a group understanding of the

meaning of the chapter in question. A good bit of time must be given to these conversations—minimally 45 minutes.

4. Students, armed with the mutually developed understanding of the chapter, then do their individually written reflections, making sure to include how the reading of the text may connect to their own lives. The teacher responds to students' reflections individually. This corresponds to the Personal and Critical phases.

5. Finally, the students reflect on a possible action to take together in response to their group's deliberations. This could include action research, community investigation, service learning or any other project developed in consultation with the teacher. This corresponds to the Creative phase.

First and Second Language Development

Helping students become the authors of their own narratives (Ricoeur, 1992) is also a powerful exercise for continuing to develop fluency in English or a home language at every stage of language development. It can be adapted to any age level, and for those not yet literate, responses can be dictated. It is also a powerful tool for engaging parents in reflective dialogue.

Reflection

Empowerment teaching and the development of cross-cultural communicative competence reaffirms each one's interconnectedness as mutually concerned members in the global family. In mediating between reflection and action within the context of schools, educators can make a path toward a compassionate and hopeful future.

References

Ada, A. F. (1995). Foreword. In J. Frederickson (Ed.), *Reclaiming our voices: Bilingual education, critical pedagogy & praxis*. Ontario, CA: California Association for Bilingual Education.

Ada, A. F. (1997). *Language and transformative education: A reader.* San Francisco: University of San Francisco.

Au, K. H. (1993). *Literacy instruction in multicultural settings* (p. 137). Orlando, FL: Harcourt Brace.

Ayers, W. (1997). *A kind and just parent: The children of Juvenile Court.* Boston: Beacon.

Banks, J. A. (1994). *An introduction to multicultural education.* Boston: Allyn and Bacon.

Banks, J. A., & McGee-Banks, C. A. (1989). *Multicultural education: Issues and perspectives.* Boston: Allyn and Bacon.

Bellah, R. et al. (1985). *Habits of the heart: Individualism & commitment in American life* (pp. 150, 153, 302). Berkeley: University of California Press.

Darder, A. (1991). *Culture and power in the classroom: A critical foundation for bicultural education* (p. 25). New York: Bergin & Garvey.

Dewey, J. (1916/1966). *Democracy and education.* New York: The Free Press.

Fishman, J. (1989). *Language and ethnicity in minority sociolinguistic perspective.* Clevedon, England: Multilingual Matters.

Freire, P. (1970/1990). *Pedagogy of the oppressed.* New York: Continuum.

Freire, P. (1973/1997). *Education for critical consciousness* (p. 136). New York: Continuum.

Gibbs, J. (1995). *Tribes. A new way of learning and being together.* Sausalito, CA: CenterSource Systems, LLC.

Igoa, C. (1995). *The inner world of the immigrant child.* New York: St. Martin's.

La Belle, T. J., & Ward, C. R. (1994). *Multiculturalism and education: Diversity and its impact on schools and society.* Albany: State University of New York Press.

Ladson-Billings, G. (1994). *The dreamkeepers: Successful teachers of African American children.* San Francisco: Jossey-Bass.

Lee, Mun Wah (Director). (1993). *Color of fear.* Video production produced at Stir Fry Productions, Oakland, CA.

Maguire, P. (1987). *Doing participatory research: A feminist approach.* Amherst, MA: Center of International Education.

McLaren, P. (1989). *Life in schools.* New York: Longman.

Neophytos-Richardson, A. (1997). *Cultural preservation and transformation in lives lived in three cultures: Interpreting the land of language and being among Greeks and Vietnamese.* Unpublished doctoral dissertation, University of San Francisco.

Nieto, S. (1992). *Affirming diversity. The sociopolitical context of multicultural education* (p. xxiii). White Plains, NY: Longman.

Olsen, L., & Mullen, N. A. (1990). *Embracing diversity. Teachers' voices from California's classrooms.* San Francisco: California Tomorrow.

Peyton, J. K. (1990). *Students and teachers writing together: Perspectives on journal writing.* Alexandria, VA: Teachers of English to Speakers of Other Languages.

Ricoeur, P. (1992). *Oneself as another.* (Trans. K. Blamey). Chicago: University of Chicago Press.

Shor, I. (1992). *Empowering education: Critical teaching for social change* (p. 197). Chicago: University of Chicago Press.

8

Creating Multiculturally Responsive Educational Settings for the Web

BIJAN B. GILLANI

Any higher mental function necessarily goes
through an external stage in its development
because it is initially a social function.
—VYGOTSKY (1981)

Education is a dynamic and evolving process susceptible to adaptation as the demands of the environment change. For years, such demands have been the force behind the creation of a true multicultural education. Despite this enthusiasm, multicultural education has failed to accommodate the cultural needs of students from diverse backgrounds. In my area of study, there are two main reasons for the shortcomings of multicultural education: scarcity of proper theoretical foundations and lack of appropriate tools. This chapter addresses both of these issues. First, I shall present an overview of Vygotsky's sociocognitive theory and its relation to human learning within what he calls the *zone of proximal development*. This zone will provide the theoretical framework for the proposed model for multicultural education. Second, I will discuss how the Web can be designed as an appropriate technological tool to implement Vygotsky's sociocognitive model in multicultural education.

Four Basic Principles: From Theory to Practice

Four basic principles will guide the reader from theory to practice in this chapter:

1. Children are born with an innate biological propensity to learn.
2. Children enter educational environments with their own previous knowledge.
3. Effective learning occurs when teaching environments can adapt to children's previous knowledge.
4. Actual learning is socially situated and it occurs through interaction with educational environments.

When based on these principles, education must apply much more than a one-curriculum-fits-all approach. It is a process of creating responsive educational settings for all students from diverse cultural backgrounds. The educational process should include a variety of teaching models and different teaching strategies to initially create a learning environment that complements the previous knowledge and the culture children bring to school with them. As children become acquainted with their new social, cultural, and educational environments, then the goal of education is to create a bridge that successfully connects students' previous knowledge with the more dominant culture of the society.

Such a dynamic educational process has been the goal of most multicultural education development in the United States; another has been economics (Cartwright, 1987). In order for the United States to retain a competitive edge, it is vital to train all U.S. students in such a way that they can truly function in the more dominant culture while they retain their own cultural values. Without proper multicultural education, students are deprived of achieving their potential development for career opportunities, thus resulting in personal, social, and economic losses.

The Need for a Multicultural Foundation

Unfortunately, despite the significant role multicultural education can play in the economic vitality of the United States and years of moral and financial support for such programs, multicultural education has failed to achieve its goals. The failure is not due to the lack of effort put forth by educators and parents, or by lack of financial support. Rather, the failure of such a system rests on how learning theories have been applied to the foundations of multicultural education, and the scarcity of appropriate tools to carry out its goals.

This chapter will address both of these issues. Vygotsky's sociocognitive theory will be discussed as a model for multicultural education. The focus will then be on the process of design for the Web as an appropriate technological tool to apply Vygotsky's sociocognitive theory (1978, 1992) to create multiculturally responsive educational environments. Finally, a Web-based example for multicultural education based on Vygotsky's theory will be presented. To meet these objectives, the following steps will be discussed in this chapter:

1. Student-centered curriculum
2. Social formation of the mind
3. Social teaching models
4. Educational features of the Web
5. The Web as a responsive tool for multicultural education
6. A thematic multicultural Web-based unit

A Student-Centered Curriculum

The key to a successful education for all students is to take each student's background into consideration. Combs, Avila, and Purkey (1971) explain that the more relevant the curriculum is to the individual, the more meaningful the learning and retention process becomes. Figure 8.1 illustrates such a process. The farther the events are from the inner perception of the students, the less effect they have on the learning process. The closer the events are to the inner perception of the students, the more likely they will change behavior, learning, and retention. To make education meaningful, Comb and other humanistic psychologists (Maslow, 1968; Rogers, 1983) suggest personalization of curriculum, or student-centered curriculum. Student-centered curriculum design should include students' social characteristics, communication styles, personality, cognitive ability, linguistic style, and academic background. These personal attributes are gained through developmental periods and they form children's inner perception about themselves and the world in which they live.

The challenge is to design curriculum that is flexible and adaptable to an individual student's inner perception. Curriculum personalization is not an easy task, because it requires enormous

FIGURE 8.1   Meaning and the Self

Source: Adapted from Combs, Avila, and Purkey (1971).

preparation time, diverse tools, and an in-depth knowledge about the diverse personal backgrounds of all students. However, as technology advances—especially the Web, with its unique, flexible, interactive, and adaptive characteristics—curriculum personalization becomes a reality.

One of the main objections to curriculum personalization is that it is impossible to personalize education for all students because there are too many unique characteristics. The issue of infinite characteristics of all students can be considered from a psychological perspective called *modal personality* (Bock, 1988), or the most common traits within cultural groups. Therefore, curriculum personalization concepts discussed in this chapter are based on modal personality rather than purely individual personality.

Before discussing design ramifications that the Web offers multicultural education, it is important to understand how children acquire their modal personality, which includes social characteristics, communication styles, personality, cognitive ability, linguistic style, and academic background.

Social Formation of the Mind

One of the most robust and original social theories with tremendous implications for multicultural education and the Web as a social tool was postulated by Vygotsky (1978, 1992). A salient feature of Vygotsky's notion is that human development and learning (e.g., social characteristics, communication styles, personality, cognitive ability, linguistic style, and academic background) originate and develop out of social and cultural interaction within what he calls the *zone of proximal development*. This zone will provide the theoretical framework for the proposed model in this chapter. A brief overview of four major themes that occur in Vygotsky's work is vital to understanding the zone of proximal development. These themes are as follows:

1. *Genetic Basis of Development:* Vygotsky distinguished between two types of mental functions: natural and higher. The *natural*

functions are the result of biological evolution. These functions are characterized by immediate responses to stimuli from the environment. The *higher* mental functions develop during ontogeny as the result of social and cultural influences that transform natural function into more complex and higher or sociocognitive functions. Cognitive development is therefore socially situated. Because humans are born with an innate genetic predisposition to respond to the environment, the individual mind reaches out into the social and cultural context and derives specific social patterns, or "modal personality," that are unique to a given society. In such a manner, the interactive social experiences become an integral part, during maturation, in shaping the individual mind to reflect the values of the society in which the individual lives. In effect, the society forms the individual mind rather than the mind being internally driven in its own construction.

2. *The Role of Language in Cognitive Development:* Internalization of higher psychological functions does not occur in a vacuum. Rather, tools of the mind mediate the transfer of cognition from the social to the individual level. Language as a tool of mind plays the most crucial role in transformation of natural functions to higher psychological functions. Just as technical tools play an essential role in shaping the physical environment, language as a symbolic tool plays a corresponding role on the internal construction of knowledge or cognition, which is culturally and socially situated.

3. *Internalization of External Activities:* Internal restructuring of external social patterns is what Vygotsky refers to as *internalization*. Vygotsky (1978, 1992) has argued that a child's development cannot be understood by a study of the individual. One must also examine the external, social, and historical world in which the individual's life develops. Development is a collaborative enterprise between the members of the society and the child. Each member of the society assists the child by providing a learning environment that enables the child's cognitive development. As will be discussed in the process of Web design, any curriculum design in school must include these personal inner

perceptions. Furthermore, in order for multicultural education to be successful, curriculum should include design features that bridge these personal inner perceptions to the values of the more dominant culture.

4. *Knowledge Formation within the Zone of Proximal Development:* Internalization of social patterns into psychological learning is best explained within the confines of what Vygotsky calls the zone of proximal development. It is within this zone that social characteristics, communication styles, personality, cognitive ability, linguistic style, and academic knowledge are transmitted from external social activities into internal psychological knowledge.

Vygotsky believed that the relationship between learning and development is a dynamic process that begins from the moment of birth and continues during the school years and beyond. Such a dynamic process has at least two levels that relate to development: One level is what the child can do on her or his own. The second is what the child is capable of achieving if the appropriate environment and assistance are provided. In other words, the child has the potential of doing more if assisted.

Looking at the relationship between learning and development from Vygotsky's point of view allows a dynamic interaction between the child and the social environment where instruction and learning are actually causing development of functions that are in the process of being developed but in need of external stimuli. Figure 8.2 shows the concept of the zone of proximal development as a recursive learning and developmental process where actual devel-

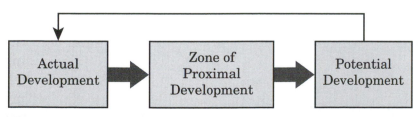

FIGURE 8.2   The Zone of Proximal Development

opment is transformed into potential development with assistance from other members of the society.

Social Teaching Model

Transformation of actual development to potential development in the zone of proximal development is not a static, abrupt, or haphazard event. Rather, children progress through roughly four sequential phases where there is a gradual internalization of social patterns to psychological patterns (Tharp & Gallimore, 1992; Gillani, 1993; Gillani & Relan, 1997). These phases are:

- Reliance on others
- Interaction with others
- Self-reliance
- Internalization

Educational Features of the Web

With the explosion of the Web as an instructional delivery medium, multicultural educators are in a unique position to deliver instruction that fits the diversity of the students. The Web is an ideal tool for applying Vygotsky's theory and the social teaching model ascribed in the previous section. For example, the Web allows the following:

- Flexibility to offer different educational activities
- Adaptability to the needs of students from diverse backgrounds
- Chat area for social interaction and communication
- Forum area for threaded discussion to provide assistance
- FTP (file transfer protocol) capability for collaboration in projects
- Electronic mail for immediate feedback
- Bulletin board for providing information and generating new ideas

- Multimedia rich content for culturally specific educational units
- Database for automated assessment
- Database application for managing students' information
- Relational database for dynamic Web lesson creation
- Live audio and video conferencing to add the human touch

Most educational Websites today do little more than present text-based content. These traditional educational approaches, dressed up in a new medium of delivery, do not provide a revolutionary improvement in education. A great majority of Web developers, including the professional ones, have yet to unlock the advantages that the Web has to offer.

The Web, ultimately, is a flexible multimedia communication network that can combine content presentation, interactive communication, research for further learning, and a production tool for students' hands-on activities. These four features of the Web (presentation, communication, research, and production) fit appropriately with the four phases of the zone of proximal development for delivering educational content. Furthermore, because of the flexibility of the Web, the diverse modal personality needs of students can be embedded into the interface design so that students with diverse backgrounds can feel at home, and therefore at ease.

Following is a design process for the Web that is multiculturally compatible. It is not a cookbook to teach HTML (Hypertext Mark Up Language) to develop Web pages. There are thousands of books and articles available that teach HTML. Rather, the following is a systematic design process that embeds Vygotsky's sociocognitive theory and its model of teaching in its approach to create an effective educational Website that is multiculturally responsive.

Design Process for the Web as a Responsive Tool for Multicultural Education

Designing and developing an effective Website to enhance multicultural instruction should follow a systematic process that includes four phases:

- Cultural analysis
- Content organization for a culturally responsive Website
- Development of multicultural Website
- Evaluation

Cultural Analysis

In the cultural analysis phase, the modal personality needs of the targeted students are identified, including their social characteristics, communication styles, personality, cognitive ability, linguistic style, and academic background. Students' cultural analysis is critical to designing an effective Website. With the students' needs and characteristics established, you can thoughtfully structure the site to reflect their modal personality needs. The analysis also provides essential information for the next phase of Web design, which is content organization for a culturally responsive Website. Learning about the cultural background of students involves the following:

1. Become involved—that is, become a member in the community about which you are seeking information. There are numerous communities—such as the church, workplace, art shows, ethnic festivals, social groups, support groups, and social services— where you can assume an active role. Once you have become part of that group, read magazines and focus journals about that group to become acquainted with their cultural patterns. Then, you should assume the role of an anthropologist and create surveys and interviews to gain information about your students' social and cultural patterns.

2. Seek information about the cultural dimensions of your students, their social characteristics, communication styles, personalities, cognitive abilities, linguistic styles, and academic backgrounds. In order to create a multiculturally responsive Website, interview the community members about these cultural dimensions and plan the design of your Website accordingly. For example, Shade, Kelly, and Oberg (1997) provide guidelines for African American and Mexican American cultural characteristics that contribute to the design of multicultural classrooms (see Table 8.1). The same type of knowledge

about students' characteristics and their cultural dimensions from other cultures is vital to the design of the Web for multicultural purposes.

TABLE 8.1   African American and Mexican American Cultural Characteristics

African American Cultural Style	*Mexican American Cultural Style*
Aesthetic appreciation of bright colors, fashionable clothing, and hair styles as the need to express their self-identity	Identifies closely with community, family, and ethnic group
A deep respect for spirituality and humanness that is often manifested through religion	Sensitive to the feelings of others
A spontaneity and ability for improvisation and rhythmic orientations shown in dance, music, and verbal and nonverbal communication	Clearly defined and respected status and role definitions within the community and family
Value system that incorporates not only the desire for success but also group unity, freedom, and equality	Achievement or success that is highly dependent on the cooperative efforts of individuals rather than competitive individualism
Socialization experiences that develop a preference for cooperation and supportiveness, which manifests itself in group affiliation	
A highly developed skill to understand and correctly perceive the affective dimensions of people and situations	

Source: Adapted from Shade, Kelly, and Oberg (1997).

3. Recognize the design implications from your findings about the students' cultural dimensions. This type of information forms the building blocks of multiculturally compatible Websites. Based on the cultural profiles of the students, consider the following questions to prepare for the next design phase:

   a. What interface design features will represent the students' cultural dimensions?
   b. What instructional model should be implemented?
   c. How should the information be structured?
   d. How should students communicate?
   e. What level of interactivity is needed?
   f. What linguistic style is appropriate?
   g. What kinds of graphics are culturally appropriate?
   h. What kinds of media best represent the culture?

Content Organization for Culturally Responsive Website

In the content organization phase, you translate the results of the students' cultural analysis into planning the look, feel, content, and relationship of educational materials. This phase includes planning and organizing for interface design (look and feel), content presentation (educational materials), and site architecture (relationship).

Interface Design

Interface design refers to the look and feel of the Website that includes the screen design, navigational tools, and interactivity. The styles of graphic presentations, color selection, placement of audio, types of video, the menu system, the navigational elements, and other elements of interface design play essential roles in the design of culturally compatible Websites.

One of the main objectives of multicultural education is to create a learning environment that fits the actual knowledge and culture students bring to school with them. By choosing the right design for the interface, you can provide the look and feel of the Web pages that reflect the diverse cultures of students.

How do you make the elements of interface design personally appealing to different cultural groups? The answer should be based on the results of the cultural analysis during the first phase. Once the information about the students' cultural dimensions has been gathered, the interface can be designed, opening opportunities for students to see themselves in their own culture. In his book, *Global Interface Design,* Fernandes (1995) provides the following three areas that need particular attention:

- Language
- Visual communication
- Appropriateness of features

When properly designed, the Web is a flexible and adaptive tool. The same Website can be designed so that different languages present the same educational content. For example, the interface design of the first page of a multiculturally responsive Website can provide buttons representing different linguistic backgrounds. Clicking on the appropriate button will navigate students to the pages where instruction is presented with the appropriate language.

Visual communication is the second area suggested by Fernandes (1995) for interface design to be culturally responsive. Visual communication refers to different elements of interface design. When designing culturally responsive interfaces, consider using the following visual communication tools:

- Employ video and audio multimedia. For example, all students have music that they enjoy. Mexican Americans may enjoy music very different from African Americans or this may be a common thread for bringing together various ethnic groups. Include audio and/or video as an element of interface design.
- Design cooperative centers, including shared areas such as chat rooms and forums for cooperative work on the Web pages.
- Create lockers for long- and short-term projects. Most students like to have storage areas, such as lockers, back packs, or briefcases. It gives them ownership of their work. In a similar manner, lockers can be presented on the interface by icons, graphics, or buttons that connect to an actual folder on the server. In this

manner, the interface acts as a locker for students to save their work. The actual saving and transferring of student's works is done through the FTP capability of the Web.

- Use of color should be in the background selection, art work, artifact, and lesson presentation. Freedom to choose colors may give the various cultural groups a feeling of ownership and being home.
- Use cultural centers. For example, create a chat area as an element of interface where students of the same cultural background can share information. (The students should also be encouraged to visit other cultural centers on the Web pages, however.)

Content Presentation

Content presentation is the effective presentation of educational materials on the Web that adheres to the educational needs of the students. As a multimedia social tool, the Web allows content presentation, interactive communication, research for further learning, and a production tool for hands-on activities. As a sociocultural learning tool, students begin to share opportunities to create centers for problem solving, interacting, communicating, and reacting to the causes of the situation they create.

Evaluation

The evaluation process determines the extent to which you have achieved the expected educational outcomes. Evaluation is a continuous process. It starts from the initial phase and continues even after the site has been developed and published. For an example of sites established, see the multiculturally responsive site at <http://etleads.csuhayward.edu/multied>. Send comments to <bgillani@csuhayward.edu>.

References

Bock, P. K. (1988). *Rethinking psychological anthropology: Continuity and change in the study of human action.* New York: W. H. Freeman.

Cartwright, C. (1987, August 15). Minority enrollment trends have national economic impact. *Black Issues in Higher Education 4,* pp. 1–2.

Combs, A. W., Avila, D. L., & Purkey, W. W. (1971). *Helping relationships: Basic concepts for the helping professions.* Boston: Allyn and Bacon.

Fernandes, T. (1995). *Global interface design: A guide to designing international user interfaces.* Boston: Academic Press.

Gillani, B. B. (1993). *Application of Vygotsky's social cognitive theory to the design of instructional materials.* Unpublished doctoral dissertation. University of Southern California.

Gillani, B. B., & Relan, A. (1997). Incorporating interactivity and multimedia into web-based instruction. In B. Khan (Ed.), *Web-based instruction.* New York: Educational Technology Publication.

Horton, W. (1994). *Designing and writing online documentation.* New York: John Wiley.

Johnson, D. W., & Johnson, R. T. (1994). Cooperative learning in the culturally diverse classroom. In R. A. DeVillar, C. J. Faltis, & J. P. Cummins (Eds.), *Cultural diversity in schools: From rhetoric to practice* (pp. 57–73). Albany: State University of New York Press.

Joyce, B., Wei, M., & Showers, B. (1992). *Models of teaching.* Boston: Allyn and Bacon.

Maslow, A. H. (1968). *Toward a psychology of being* (2nd ed.). New York: Van Nostrand.

Rogers, C. R. (1983). *Freedom to learn for the 80s.* Columbus, OH: Merrill.

Shade, B. J., Kelly, C., & Oberg, M. (1997). *Creating culturally responsive classrooms.* Washington, DC: American Psychological Association.

Suchman, R. J. (1962). *The elementary school training program in scientific inquiry.* (Report to the U.S. Office of Education, Project Title VII.) Urbana, IL: University of Illinois.

Tharp, R. G., & Gallimore, R. (1988). *Rousing minds of life: Teaching, learning, and schooling in context.* New York: Cambridge University Press.

Vygotsky, L. S. (1978). *Mind in society: The development of higher psychological processes* (M. Cole, V. John-Steiner, S. Scribner, & E. Soubermann, Eds. & Trans.). Cambridge, MA: MIT Press.

Vygotsky, L. S. (1981). The genesis of higher mental functions. In J. V. Wertsch (Ed.), *The concept of activity in Soviet psychology.* Armonk, NY: Sharpe.

Vygotsky, L. S. (1992). *Thought and language* (A. Kozulin, Ed. & Trans.). Cambridge, MA: MIT Press.

9

Schools and Families
What Is Transformative Collaboration?

NANCY JEAN SMITH

My family is more important to me than anything else, and that includes school.—FOURTH-GRADE STUDENT

It was an early summer evening. Night was swiftly falling and we were nearing the end of a peaceful and lovely gathering of my students and their parents to commemorate my departure from their school district. I was uncharacteristically quiet, while my gleeful kindergartners and their siblings and friends were running wildly about me, weaving circles between their families and myself, shouting loudly in Spanish and in English. And there I was, the speechless Gringo Bilingual "Spanish-speaking" kindergarten teacher. In the form of a larger circle were all my students' Mexican migrant parents, many aunts and uncles, even some grandparents and friends, all looking anxious and waiting for me to speak, to provide some answers. "Can you still help us now that you will not be working in the district?" a parent asked.

Encircling me, each one in turn had given me the gift of their voice, words of encouragement, thanks, and advice. However, I was totally taken by surprise when the last two parents asked, "Maestra, what I would really like you to tell us is . . . well . . . How do we go about working with the principal?" I wasn't sure what they were asking. No words would come. His wife continued also in Spanish, "But that's not enough, how do we change how the superintendent thinks about us and how do we get ourselves elected to the Board of Education?" I felt uneasy, yet excited by the questions. I knew what was taking place was profound and would cause me great pondering, but the last question also left me with a sinking unnerved feeling: Was I leaving them just when they needed me? I was not prepared for the depth of their thought, but I should have been. The year-long work we had done led them to these questions. My voice was silent, yet they pressed on.

It was a magical moment, one of those recollections that forever nourishes my spirit of solidarity and resistance, and even today continues to provide me with the needed strength to refuse an easy, mundane, and trivial road to educating all children.

Democratic Teaching in a Traditional Setting

In this chapter I will discuss the corroborating factors that made this project highly successful. Action-oriented collaboration between parents and teachers was our goal and outcome so that parents could become protagonists of their children's education. My purpose in this chapter is to relate those experiences to effective democratic teaching practices and specifically to look at how home/school interaction can create culturally responsive partnerships. Finally, I will end with a checklist of questions designed to examine this struggle and reflect on transformative teaching practices.

Examining Personal Assumptions: The Place to Start

To be adequately prepared to teach all students, teachers must honestly question their personal cultural assumptions and social influences that directly affect their pedagogy and all areas of schooling they impart daily to their students. It is imperative that teachers develop a sensitivity toward their personal implication in the social conditions that create or destroy full democratic participation in schools and that they continually focus on understanding how to make meaning of one's everyday life. In other words, educators must understand and see very clearly what their identity and culture is, and how it intersects with their students' and their families' cultures and identities.

Good multicultural teaching means continually developing sensitivity, which is equally important for a teacher in a diverse classroom as a teacher in a monocultural classroom. All children need role models that can model appropriate inclusive behavior and show them through daily dialogue how to take responsibility for their own learning. It is imperative that a teacher be able to recognize and teach that assumptions matter and that one's culture affects those assumptions. Out of that sensitivity, teachers may then recognize the need for further information in order to help them make sense of their students' world.

Acknowledging Privilege

The most difficult place to start in creating democratic culturally responsive educators is with one's soul. This is the hardest quest in effective multicultural education because it requires compassionate vigilance toward privilege and sometimes painful acknowledgments. As people take in new knowledge, they also need to nurture and contemplate kindness, peace, and love to themselves and their doubts.

I mention this here because as this project is unfolded in this chapter, it is important to note that none of this would have occurred if I had not also been at all times on the road of questioning, information searching, reflection, and self-vigilance. In other words, I was a teacher and a researcher. I was analyzing and researching my teaching and learning environment at the same time that I was teaching and learning myself!

An extremely useful tool in all this work is a reflective journal. It can help sort out reactions and point one toward one's inner thoughts. The journal that I quote from in this chapter kept me focused on what was working and helped me face fears that were difficult to name in any other way. Just like many other teachers, I was marching along with this project with very little outside guidance.

Building Trust

Nosotros los immigrantes queremos que los maestros enseñan nuestros hijos como tratar a la gente, sobre todo el respeto a las personas mayores. El respeto es lo mas importante en mi pueblo. Aqui en los Estados Unidos no saben respetar. Yo quisiera que mi hija sea como la gente de mi pueblo, donde saludan a las personas cuando se encuentran en la calle. En mi pueblo no hay gente invisible.—JAVIER MENDOZA, ARTIST / FARMER / FACTORY WORKER, 24 YEARS OLD

[Translation] We immigrants, we want teachers to teach our children to be good to others, and above all to respect their elders. Respect is the most important thing in my village. People in the United States don't know how to respect. I hope that my daughter will grow up in the ways of those from my village, where everyone greets one another on the street. In my village there are no invisible people.

It is easy to say, and easy to know, that the place to start in building a relationship with students' parents is trust. But how does a teacher actually "do" this, when many teachers do not share the culture or important common knowledge of their students, let alone live in the community in which they teach? What are the walls that exist between schools and families, and how does one identify how these walls were created? Breaking down walls between parents, students, and educators requires dialogue, and it takes place in calculated and sometimes small steps.

Beginning Dialogue

In my experiences in working with Mexican migrant parents, I had noticed that my parents valued Mexican dance. As I began the year, I thought about how well attended the Cinco de Mayo events are every year. I wondered if dance could be a unifying theme/project in which my parents and students would be interested. I went into a research mode and from the first day of school began asking parents if they would like to help with dance during the year. I received no religious objections—only smiles and tentative yeses. I talked up the idea with the parents who came by my room and tried to engage parents in discussions of what they knew about dance. It seemed to bring back many memories of their childhood that they liked talking about and it seemed to make them feel comfortable. Establishing dialogue takes a lot of time.

Continuing to Build Dialogue

Then came Back to School Night. I decided to formally launch a dance project idea with the parents. Purposely I set up the room in small groups so that parents would be facing one another easier than they would be facing me as I spoke, and facilitated the evening with the purpose in mind that they would get to know one another. Less than one-quarter of the parents showed, and they came in at different times, but as each one came to my door, I smiled and explained (and reexplained!) what we were talking about. I never left anyone out, and always stopped to recognize any new parent. They discussed with one another where they were from and the dances that they enjoyed during their school years. I asked one of them to record this information for me. They shared their information back to the group and I put it into a semantic map. It was a simple exercise but very effective, and we were able to move on to my idea of a year-long dance project. We brainstormed how much money we would need, how to raise the money, and what roadblocks we might expect to encounter. Finally, a date was set (upon my insistence) for the following month, October, to continue planning.

Risk Taking and Its Rewards

Meanwhile, I did not wait until the October meeting to take action. I enrolled myself in a local Mexican dance group that met once a week. I felt a bit awkward because I was not Mexican, but pushed forward because I knew it was for my students. As the October meeting came closer, I continued to remind the parents of our meeting. I called those I did not see regularly and talked up the idea with the children. It helps to put on dance music in class and discuss dance, costumes, and gestures, and to talk about it as much as possible so that they would also be excited and remind their parents.

The October meeting was attended by many of the same parents who came to Back to School Night, but some of them brought another parent with them. After school, I spent time talking with the parents who came to my door, and purposely trying to engage various parents in conversations together. I noticed that in a couple of cases the friend they brought to the meeting was the same friendship I had also been fomenting. The meeting was slow, and it was decided that another meeting of all the parents was necessary in order to make a final yes or no decision on the project. An uncomfortable feeling began to grow in my mind at this time, such as, "Maybe they really do not want this project, and I am just pushing it on everyone."

Parent Participation: A Tiny Step at a Time

A note about a late October meeting was sent out to all the parents two weeks later, and I continued to work on building friendships with the parents. Anytime anyone would show up at my door, I would stop class, invite that parent in, and ask if he or she could stay to help with class. If they were busy at that time, I would press for when they could come back. It was important to me that they knew they were important in our classroom, and that they were welcome and needed.

The night of the late October meeting, I had a conflict with the School Site Council meeting and left that meeting early for ours. As I waited with the principal for people to show for the School Site Council meeting, I took the opportunity to describe to him the dance project in detail. I had left my room open and when I walked over there for the meeting, I was pleasantly surprised. The room was packed! There was hardly standing room. As the meeting unfolded, it was obvious that some prior discussions had taken place and that parents had already made supportive decisions.

That year, we raised $1,700 and outfitted all the children in dance clothing made by the parents. We spent a chunk of the money to have collective and individual pictures taken, which each student received. To this day, if I go into the homes of my former students, those pictures are hanging on the walls of their parents' homes. At the end of the year, the principal came to me and said that we could not walk in the Cinco de Mayo parade because of the heat. I was able to gather the parents together with the news and they found and organized the decorating of a flatbed truck. We took first place in the parade!

In Retrospect

Now, to return to the scenario at the beginning of this chapter: I obviously had done some things right, had gained the parents' trust, and had connected the school to their lives. As a result, I found that the parents now trusted me with their inner thoughts and I felt unsure of how to interact with the questions that were being posed to me. I did not have answers and I felt as if I were letting them down. My feelings were those of confusion as my mind raced, grasping to understand the depth of the interaction that was passing before me. There were suddenly no words in my mouth to express the fullness in my heart. Physically, the tightness in my throat and my chest would not allow for speech to come forth. Instead, what came out were tears of pain, tears of fear, tears of joy, but mostly, tears of hope. I choked and told them it was not me they needed; those who were needed had been working with them all year.

The Students

Connecting Curriculum to Homelife

Every step of the way, I looked for ways to connect classroom dialogue, homework, and curriculum to family knowledge and family existence. The students and I made books about why they wanted to dance, which gave them a chance to explore their desire to make their parents happy. In many of the books, the children found themselves physically present in the pictures; in one book, we even put photographs of each child dancing. In this way, the children had the opportunity to see themselves represented in a book, with text of their own words. They saw that the words that they spoke are the words that we write, and that the life that we live is content for a book. Similarly, the parents recorded their early memories and childhood experiences in books, often illustrated by the children. These books, even today, adorn coffee tables and occupy prominent spaces in the homes of many students. They are heritage treasures that will surely be shared with grandchildren.

It is imperative that classwork help children make connections with what they know as they reach out to less familiar and unknown territory. With the parents' help, we made maps of the world, maps of Mexico, and maps of the various dance regions we had been studying. I wanted the children to know that the dance we were learning was just one of many, many others, and that those many others represented a richness in their cultural heritage. All of these assignments—whether homework or in-class projects—built family knowledge. Even if a teacher does not speak the language of the family, he or she can still foment interaction and respect for family knowledge as a base for academic work. Finding ways for children to feel pride for their parents and families is critical to their academic success. It also builds on the teacher's curriculum work, because having parents share orally and in writing gives the teacher the opportunity to explain deeper understandings of literacy as well as expand the parents' view of literacy. This will help them work more effectively with their children in gaining speed and efficiency in English and content knowledge.

Interactive Journals

Interactive journals that are sent home and come back to the teacher allow a three-way conversation to take place and facilitate immediate messages to pass back and forth. As trust is built with the parents, a conversation becomes possible that enables the project to move forward. Many of the parents commented later that it was exciting to see what the teacher had written to them that day.

Finally, in expanding a paradigm on curriculum, it is helpful to remember to integrate the music of the home through the use of songbooks as a language arts curriculum base. We wrote out the words to the songs we were dancing to, decorated them in poster style, and created songbooks with our favorite music. This moved beyond superficial multicultural music appreciation into the arena of curriculum. That is solid inclusive teaching—the deepest structure of multicultural education that allows the students the space to discuss prejudice in musical terms. In essence, it allows movement toward antiracist teaching.

Arriving at Dialogue

This memory that I have shared of parents coming together has repeated itself in many social forms, and carries with it the threat of change, the retribution from those who fear solidarity, the danger of empowerment, and the vulnerability of families acting as agents of their own destiny. These qualities can be difficult to deal with when working from within an educational "institution," but as can be easily seen, the need is great to actively foment efficacy if teachers wish to develop meaningful school and familial relationships. Teachers must face the contradictions that exist and prepare themselves for messy answers if schools are to be responsive to the diverse needs of students and their families.

In *Reclaiming Our Voices,* Frederickson (1995) talks about the fact that each human being knows something and that by believing that each human brings a special knowledge to the table opens the possibility for dialogue to take place. Dialogue, then, is the goal with parents, for open, caring, loving, and equitable relations to develop. It is through dialogue that educators can construct a solid education for all children. Without dialogue, the possibilities for optimal relations and outcomes are lost.

Believing That All Parents Are Constructors of Knowledge

The strength of this project lies in the fact that it builds on parenting skills already in place. It supports a sincere concern for the future educational success and happiness of their children. It views working collectively as a family unit as opposed to working independently. Most importantly, there exists a belief in the parents' capabilities of helping their children at home and becoming involved at school. When validated parents become self-assured, they begin to question school policy in the arenas of language, instruction, and so on. Becoming more aware of the educational system is what motivated these parents to speak out, to say their mind openly.

Looking carefully, one can see that the direction of learning flows from school to child, child to parent, and parent to teacher in a completely dialectical fashion that creates a forum for the development of authentic democratic relationships. When the flow of knowledge production is no longer linear, a dialectic of what might be can emerge, and the standard operating model no longer rules modes of behavior and operation. Parents feel encouraged to negotiate and analyze different realities. That is why the parents in my classroom were willing to take the risk and say their words aloud. This clearly demonstrates that a strong parent-involvement program not only plays a significant role in the parents' personal development but is likewise a critical factor in the success of their children's school existence.

Families are the foundation of society, and children are the connection to the future. This is the basis of a profound understanding that education all too frequently overlooks in practice. When one honestly contemplates the situation that a vast number of families encounter the English language and a dominant mainstream culture as alien to their own language and culture, one easily recognizes the wide gulf that exists between school and homelife. There are important pieces of the home/school connection missing, and they will remain missing until an inclusive infrastructure is formed.

As the children and all those involved with their schooling cry out for curriculum that holds potential to heal families and society, educators must investigate carefully and then act on the potentiality that parent partnerships hold out for rethinking curriculum. The issues of inclusion and how the nation is educating its youths must be critically examined.

When a community is homogeneous, monocultural schools are a logical extension. However, when ethnic diversity is represented physically yet invisibly in school culture, then someone is being left out. Today, school populations are obviously diverse from the school staff. This requires that a reevaluation of the educational process and of school culture and curricula occur. It also implies that schools find ways to reach out, build trust, and celebrate all communities beyond food and fiesta events. To create a genuinely better society, it is vital that all voices be included in the ongoing construction. Critical to this whole process is the necessity that educators be inclusionary with families and parents and watch thoughtfully to ensure that schools celebrate and reflect the community that they serve in ways beyond the superficial.

Relating My Stories to Your Stories

I have shared one of my teaching stories, not as a model project to be replicated, but rather as an example to be taken apart, to be thought about carefully. I followed my heart and actively worked to build bridges with my community. When I began, I had many questions of which I was very unsure, but most surprising to me was that at the end I had even more questions! In many cases, I felt helplessly lacking in the tools to go about helping my families. However, if you are willing to let the questions guide you and to ask yourself the hard, sometimes painful, questions in dialogue, then you can be assured to at least be on the path to somewhere together with your families.

So ask yourself some hard questions, and add to the list that I have begun here. The following are meant to guide your thoughts concerning your own projects and pedagogical directions. Critical multicultural teaching is not easy, but articulating and problem posing inclusiveness is a strong beginning.

Go Ahead and Dig in with Some Hard Questions

1. Why is getting to know one another such an important building block?
2. What strategies did I use that encouraged parents to get to know one another and move into dialogue?
3. What other strategies can you use to build community at each opportunity? Could this project be done with older students? Would a teacher go about recruiting parents in the same way or are there differences for an older students and parents?

4. Even if you do not speak the language of your students' parents, how can you create bridges with families, and not foment distance?
5. How can you help parents and students see their lives as a basis for daily curriculum?
6. What are some of the tough questions that this chapter has brought to your mind?

Reference

Frederickson, J. (1995). *Reclaiming our voices.* Ontario, CA: California Association for Bilingual Education.

10

Transformation of "At-Risk" Identity
Parental Involvement and Resiliency Promotion

R. GREG JENNINGS

Words have the power to destroy or heal. When words are both true and kind, they can change our world.—J. KORNFIELD (1994)

I see the words *at-risk child* as oppressive, hope robbing, and limiting. The label refers to the probability that one might experience some negative future outcome based on a current level of stress. Unfortunately, children and their families who are considered to be "at risk" (for what is rarely identified) are frequently assumed to be minority, poor, and passively victimized. The *at-risk* label is a media-convenient explanation for failure among children that blames *them* for their failure (Miron, 1996). Victimization denies *agency* (hooks, 1995). Terms of victimization, such as *at-risk chil-dren,* evoke media attention, yet the emphasis on the oppressive issues negates the ability of the oppressed to generate change and to seek allies. Specifically, a victim-focused identity often emerges when a person believes that she or he cannot be treated equally. Given limited inner coping resources, the victim role is often seen as the only way to seek equity and resources.

> *Question:* How does one foster a genuine sense of agency among children and their families in this area of "at-risk" labeling?

On the other side of risk, I see *resiliency,* the capacity to bounce back from adversities, as one important transformative concept. Every person is at risk for something. Yet children who have the social support of caring adults and the ability to reapprise their experiences, including those that are traumatic, are more likely to heal and to grow stronger (Katz, 1997). I do not mean to minimize the impact of grim, unequal, and ineffective educational environ-ments, as vividly described in Kozol's (1991) *Savage Inequalities.* Rather, I intend to focus on those words and concepts that help edu-cators to recognize children's potential to somehow transform these environments into resources, as illustrated in Katz's (1997) *On Playing a Poor Hand Well.*

Hardships as well as triumphs are welcomed literary contribu-tions to the understanding of children; however, in order for chil-dren to act on their world, they need words that spark some new way of viewing their experiences. An awareness of resiliency can spark dramatic changes in children's beliefs and actions. Further, this state of resiliency can be fostered when parents, teachers, and communities work collaboratively. The challenge is to understand how to encourage meaningful partnerships between them in order to promote resiliency.

This chapter will focus on the role of parent participation in the promotion of resiliency in children. Overviews, questions, and activ-ities related to the PRIDE Model of Resiliency Promotion conclude the chapter to assist teachers in building collaboration between par-ents, schools, and communities.

Why Partnerships to Promote Resiliency?

At the beginning of this chapter, I contrasted an at-risk perspective with a resiliency perspective. When communities come together to plan, they often face a choice between "problematizing" (Freire, 1993) and "personalizing" (Haynes & Comer, 1996) the focus of their efforts. Historically, there is much to criticize about inequities in U.S. public education. A resilient perspective, however, is evident in the approach Comer and his associates have demonstrated in creating school curriculum and instruction that "nourish" children's minds and "warm" their hearts. Full, ongoing, and meaningful participation of parents in schools can result in a strength/solution focus rather than a weakness/problem orientation.

One Mother's Involvement

Mrs. Washington started a part-time job after her daughter, Alice, began the first grade. By the second grade, she began to feel dissatisfied with her role in her daughter's education and questioned if she would have much to offer her. She wanted to do more, yet she wasn't able to help out in the school during the day. During this time, a few teachers at her daughter's school began plans on a parent-taught after-school hobby and activity program. Teachers called all their students' parents to recruit planners and teachers. When Mrs. Washington received a call, her first response was, "I've never taught a class before. What can I teach?"

Her daughter's second-grade teacher, Ms. Harter, had always made time to talk with parents outside of her door after school. Lately she had gone out of her way to bring parents into her classroom. It was this welcoming into the classroom that made Mrs. Washington feel more comfortable to ask more about the after-school program. The teacher and parent talked for some time. It was evident that Mrs. Washington was very skilled in art, so Ms. Harter encouraged her to become the art teacher and to help in planning the program. She accepted the offer and taught an art class. The story doesn't end with her simply planning and teaching the class, however.

After several weeks of collaborating with other parents and experiencing leadership for the first time, Mrs. Washington applied for and attained a job as a teacher's assistant. Given her work with other parents, she was asked to serve on the school's site council committee, the group of parents that made decisions about how resources are used. Within a few months, Mrs. Washington was recruiting other parents for the council and making meaningful decisions.

(One such decision was to vote against a school proposal to use funds for classroom materials in favor of hiring an additional classrooms aide.) She also felt a new confidence in helping Alice to learn and she began seeing her own strengths in a new light.

What Influences Involvement?

In a literature review of factors influencing parental school involvement, Hoover-Dempsey and Sandler (1997) identify the following areas of parental beliefs and attitudes as significant:

1. Child development and rearing
2. Parental role in children's educational development
3. Self-efficacy in supporting learning
4. Attributions for children's success, failure, and intellectual growth
5. Problem-solving strategies

Empirically, clusters of parental beliefs—including educational attitude, grade expectation, child-rearing beliefs, and parental efficacy—have been found to be significantly related to grade attainment among Latino American and European American children (Okagahi & Frensch, 1998). Yet, parental attitude is not sufficient to ensure *meaningful* education. "The crucial issue in successful learning is not home or school—teacher or student—but the relationship between them. Learning takes place where there is a productive learning relationship" (Seeley, cited in Christenson, Rounds, and Franklin, 1992, p. 19).

What Characteristics Foster Partnerships?

Dunst, Johanson, Rounds, Trivette, and Hamby (1992) surveyed 102 educational professionals and 69 parents to identify the most important characteristics necessary for meaningful partnership. The top 10 characteristics, as rated by parents and professionals, were trust, mutual respect, open communication, honesty, active listening, openness, flexibility, caring, understanding, and shared responsibility (p. 162). Once these characteristics are demonstrated, teachers and educators have the opportunity to help parents promote resiliency through an educational partnership.

The PRIDE Model of Resiliency Promotion

This section provides an overview of the importance of the PRIDE Model to Resiliency, as well as questions for parents and children, encouragers, and activities. The process of critical questions can be a powerful method of raising children's consciousness of their roles in acting on their environment.

P lanning
R esponsibility
I nterest
D etermination
E xpectations

Planning

Children who successfully cope with stress (e.g., peer pressures, racism, educational inequities, etc.) need a strategy to most efficiently use their resources (e.g., energy, social skills, and positive thinking). To plan is to reflect on the challenges/obstacles and to prepare to respond in a way that increases the chances of overcoming them. Planning must be taught. Planning evokes a self-awareness in children that is crucial in shifting them from passive victims (objects of stress) to active agents of self change (subjects of new stories).

Questions for Parents and Children

1. If you could do something special that is really important to you, what would you do? What is special about it?
2. What would you need to do it? [Some kids need books, or art materials, or help from a teacher.]
3. What would you do first? Second? Next?
4. How long would it take? How would you know when you finished?

Encouragement

- Take some silent time today to think about how you will reach your goals.
- You can do a good job when you use your mind to plan your tasks.
- You always have a choice about how to reach your dreams.
- I like how you plan your time to learn.

Activity

Help the child choose a special project/challenge. Set up a one-week time frame to monitor the steps involved. For five minutes each day, review the preceding questions and be sure to give plenty of encouragement.

Responsibility

Children who have overcome significant environment stressors (e.g., dangerous neighborhoods) as well as familial stress (e.g., mental health concerns) frequently have opportunities to value and demonstrate responsibility, an ownership of the challenge and related strategies. This responsibility gives them a sense of purpose

(Katz, 1997). Believing that one can take charge of a problem or a challenge can be a protective attitude against stress. Parents can foster this attitude by promoting opportunities for responsibility.

> A challenge is a tough time you face that you decide to do something about.

Questions for Parents and Children

1. What have you done in the past when you had a really tough challenge? How did it work?
2. What is it like when you decide to do something about a challenge? (What would it be like if you decided to do something about a challenge?)
3. How can you take charge of a tough challenge you are facing now?
4. What could help you to be successful?

Encouragement

- When you choose to face a challenge, you get stronger in taking charge of your future.
- You are a resilient kid! You can choose to do something about the things you face!
- I'm proud of the way you "owned" the challenge. (Nobody but you took on the challenge.)
- You own the steps to your dreams.

Activity

Talk about a time in which a family member faced a challenge and decided to do something about it. Include examples of how other people helped the member to act.

Interest

Interest provides the energy for resiliency. Without an interest in or curiosity about the world, there would be little motivation for children to generate efforts to overcome challenges. Parents who understand their children's interests are able to help them see new connections between love of play, love of meaningful learning, and love of growing.

Questions for Parents and Children

1. Of all the things you do, what do you like doing the most?
2. What would make you feel really proud?
3. What would you really like to learn about? Why?
4. What excites you?

Encouragement

- Your interests are so powerful that nothing can stop you from learning and growing once you know them.
- You have the spark of life when you grow your interests!
- When you're excited, you're learning and changing your world.

Activity

Following the questions, find a family member, teacher, neighbor, or family friend who shares an interest with your child. Ask the person to share stories, books, letters, or materials related to the interest. Are there any stories about how the interest helped the person to meet challenges?

Determination

Without determination, interests may rise and fall as difficulties arise. To be resilient is to maintain a will to overcome adversities. This is an attitude that parents model on a daily basis.

Questions for Parents and Children

1. What can a person say to himself or herself when he or she feels like giving up during a challenge?
2. Whom can you go to when you are having a hard time and you feel like giving up? What could you ask this person?

3. Have you ever felt like giving up when you faced a tough challenge? What did that feel like? (Acknowledge feelings of discouragement or hopelessness.) What did you do?
4. Do you have any tough challenges now? What could you do to keep on trying your hardest even when you are tired?

Encouragement

- I believe in you.
- You can stay with your dreams even when they seem too hard.
- Everyone gets tired, discouraged, afraid, unsure, or unmotivated sometimes.
- That's the time you get to prove yourself and make yourself proud.
- Remember _____ (a family, community, or cultural hero/ heroine) when you need courage to keep working toward a goal.

Activity

Identify a family, community, or cultural hero. Share a story about how she or he demonstrated a desire to pursue a hope or dream.

Expectations

High expectations help children set a standard for their efforts. Resiliency in the face of great odds requires extraordinary efforts. Therefore, parents are central in fostering the level of effort needed to combine planning, responsibility, interest development, and determination into resilient children's daily lives.

Questions for Parents

1. What do I expect from my child (e.g., grades; reading, writing, and math skills; community, etc.)?
2. How do I let my child know what I expect?
3. How do I make sure that my expectations are realistic, yet help my child reach for higher levels?

4. What information or assistance would I like to have in order to know what to expect? (See questions in the next section to explore children's strengths and needs.)

Encouragement

- I am proud of you.
- You have many gifts and I expect you to use them.
- You are resilient and that means that I know that you can deal with your challenge even though it's tough.

Activity

Set a goal. Take five minutes a day to talk to the child about how planning, responsibility, interest, and determination are related to what you expect from him or her.

Parental Questions Fostering Resiliency through Communication

The following are questions that can aid parents in discovering and communicating strengths, desires, and challenges of their children with the school. Give these questions to children's parents as an opportunity to encourage partnership through communication at gatherings such as back-to-school nights or parent-teacher conferences.

1. I am pleased when my child _____.
2. When my child graduates from school, I want her or him to be able to _____.
3. It would help me to know more about my child's school regarding _____.
4. It would be good for my child's teacher/school to know the following about my child: _____.
5. Some of the hardest challenges/choices my child faces are _____.
6. My child has these strengths to deal with these challenges/choices: _____

7. What would I like for my child to learn to better deal with these challenges? _____

Questions for Teachers in Reflecting on Attitudes toward Parents

Darder (1997) emphasizes the importance of teachers assessing their values regarding equity as well as their biases toward cultural groups in developing a sense of cultural democracy. In addition, she calls for reflection on the perception of power (i.e., as corruptive or absolutely positive) in understanding and addressing inequities in teaching and learning. These two themes of values and power are essential in developing cultural democracy among parents as well as children. The following are questions for teachers to ask themselves when creating new approaches to instruction with school/ parent relationships in mind:

Value Assessment

1. What are some challenges I see in working with parents of the most needy students? How would I describe these parents to a colleague? *Note:* Characteristics often include:
   - Unconcerned ("Never participates or communicates," "Provides basic supplies," "Unsupportive," etc.)
   - Hostile ("Seems angry and makes me feel defensive," "Blames everyone else for problems," etc.)
   - Uneducated ("Can't help child with work," "Doesn't seem to have skills," etc.)
   - Dysfunctional ("Disorganized, late, unkept," "Seems to be 'out-there,'" etc.)
   - Overreactive ("Too critical, invested, paranoid, vocal," etc.)
2. What do these descriptions say about my view of the parents and of their children?

Power and Parenting

1. How do I help parents experience a sense of power in supporting their child's education? How might I use the following to develop

curriculum and activities that foster parent involvement and cultural democracy?

   a. Parents' goals/aspirations for their child

   b. Parents' ideas on social topics, community challenges, or unique cultural experiences

   c. Parents' possible contributions (e.g., skills, experiences, stories)

2. How do I support parents in their own education of their children (e.g., activities that elicit involvement of entire families [without penalizing levels of education] and emphasize family strengths)?

3. How do I link meaningful assignments and class activities with the values and goals of parents? How can these links then provide parents with an opportunity to communicate their hopes for their children's future parenting (metaparenting)?

4. How do I help students and parents recognize "isms" (e.g., racism, sexism, age-ism) without communicating victim identities? How can I help them connect experiences of anger and discomfort in "isms" to the need for proactive steps against "isms"?

References

Christenson, S., Rounds, T., & Franklin, M. (1992). Home-school collaboration: Effects, issues, and opportunities. In S. Christenson & J. Close Conoley (Eds.), *Home-school collaboration: Enhancing children's academic and social competence* (pp. 19–51). Silver Springs, MD: National Association of School Psychologists.

Darder, A. (1997). Creating the conditions for cultural democracy in the classroom. In A. Darder, R. Torres, & H. Gutiérrez (Eds.), *Latinos and education: A critical reader* (pp. 331–350). New York: Routledge.

Dunst, C., Johanson, C., Rounds, T., Trivette, C., & Hamby, D. (1992). Characteristics of parent-professional partnerships. In S. Christenson & J. Close Conoley (Eds.), *Home-school collaboration: Enhancing children's academic and social competence* (pp. 157–192). Silver Springs, MD: National Association of School Psychologists.

Epstein, J. L. (1987). Toward a theory of family-school connections: Teacher practices and parent involvement. In K. Hurrelmann, F. Kaufmann, & F. Losel (Eds.), *Social intervention: Potential and constraints* (pp. 121–136). New York: DeGruyter.

Freire, P. (1993). *Pedagogy of the oppressed* (3rd ed.). (Myra Bergman Ramos, Trans.). New York: Continuum.

Haynes, N., & Comer, J. (1996). Integrating schools, families, and communities through successful school reform: The school development program. *School Psychology Review 25,* pp. 501–506.

Ho, B. (1997). The school psychologist's role based on an ecological approach to family-school-community collaborations. *The California School Psychologist 2,* pp. 31–38.

hooks, b. (1995). *Killing rage: Ending racism.* New York: Holt.

Hoover-Dempsey, K., & Sandler, H. (1997). Why do parents become involved in their children's education? *Review of Educational Research 67,* pp. 3–42.

Katz, M. (1997). *On playing a poor hand well: Insights from the lives of those who have overcome childhood risks and adversities.* New York: W. W. Norton.

Kornfield, J. (1994). *Buddha's little instruction book.* New York: Bantam.

Kozol, J. (1991). *Savage inequalities: Children in america's schools.* New York: Crown.

Miron, L. (1996). *The social construction of urban schooling: Situating the crisis.* Cresskill, NJ: Hampton.

Okagaki, L., & Frensch, P. (1998). Parenting and children's school achievement: A multiethnic perspective. *American Educational Research Journal 35,* pp. 123–144.

11

From Crossing Borders to Building Bridges
The Role of Euro-American Teachers in Bilingual / Multicultural Classrooms

MARGARET C. LAUGHLIN

I have a lot to say on this topic. And I have come a long way. I am from Newport News, Virginia. (group laughter) Now you see what that brings up? . . . When you're a white male from the South? I come from a middle-class conservative family, and look where I am! I'm bilingual teaching! . . . I think that's a really cool question. How on Earth did I end up here? We have as much right to join the dialogue on multiculturalism as another ethnic group, and we can define our topic without being racist. —RYAN

Ryan, a middle school teacher, expresses the sentiment of many White teachers who happen to be working in classrooms in which they are an ethnic minority, and who spend a good portion of their day teaching in Spanish, not their native language, to native Spanish speakers. As a participant among a group of other Euro-American bilingual teachers, his words announced the beginning of an investigation, a call for White bilingual teachers to examine the nature of their work and to connect with critical perspectives that go beyond a traditional framework to define their role. Ryan's words push one to reflect on the pedagogical foundations of one's labor, and to expand the human agency of Euro-American bilingual teachers as members of an ethnic group within a multicultural society.

What does it mean to be a White person who works in a bilingual or multicultural classroom? Or as another teacher participant so simply asked, "When you ask your kids, if you do have a multicultural class, . . . to bring something from their culture to share, what do *you* bring to share?" What is the nature of one's practice as one seeks to understand the politics of language and diversity in today's schools? These are some of the questions that I have confronted in my own work, and about which I continue to hear from my students and colleagues in teacher education.

After years of teaching in multicultural classrooms, I found that my doubts and anxieties around being White, middle class, and "mainstream" found a response when I engaged in a participatory research project with seven other Euro-American bilingual teachers that began in a seminar in Oaxaca, Mexico, and continued over the subsequent year. Our pseudonyms are Nick, Elise, Nancy Jean, Jessica, Ryan, Terri, Valerie, and myself, Peggy (actually, my nickname). What came out of our work was more than can be easily summarized, nor has this labor come to a final conclusion. In this chapter, however, I will highlight the major themes or issues surrounding the practice of Euro-American bilingual teachers, how we progressed through our dialogues and reflections into recognizing the transformative potentials of our work, and what this means for other teachers entering bilingual/multicultural classrooms who may identify with the same kinds of issues.

There is a significant body of literature focusing on White teachers in multicultural education (Banks, 1995; Delpit, 1995; Hidalgo, 1993; hooks, 1994; McIntosh, 1988; Mcyntire, 1997; Nieto, 1992; Paley, 1979; Sleeter & McClaren, 1995) and a multitude of texts about bilingual teachers within various pedagogical perspectives (Ada, 1990; Canales, 1992; Cummins, 1989; Darder, 1993; Fredrickson, 1995; Freeman & Freeman, 1994; Freire, 1970, 1986, 1994; Freire & Macedo, 1987; Krashen & Biber, 1988; Quintanar-Sarellana, 1991; Scarcella, 1990; Tinajero & Ada, 1992). However, I have found there is generally a lack of adequate discussion of the perspectives of Euro-American educators who are bilingual and practicing in bilingual/multicultural programs. In no source have I found any qualitative and participatory studies conducted in collaboration with Euro-American bilingual teachers in which their own experiences are analyzed. In effect, a core of professional dialogue around the issues of White teachers within the field of bilingual education is only incidental within the larger context of multicultural education. Consequently, I could never hear my own voice when attempting to connect my own experiences with what has been put out there to prepare us for the multiple dimensions of our work.

Why Would the Issues of Euro-American Bilingual Teachers Be of Concern?

The majority of teaching and preservice teaching populations in the United States are from White, middle-class background, whereas the number of students from non-White or non-English–speaking backgrounds is significant and growing (Chisholm, 1994). The fastest growing and largest group of language minority students speak Spanish as their first language, whereas the number of qualified Spanish bilingual teachers remains inadequate to provide support to those students learning English. This narrative serves to underscore and validate the experiences of White, middle-class teachers who are striving to become proficient in the language and culture of their students, who are experiencing successes and failures, and who are frequently exposed to political controversy and scrutiny within their school communities.

These teachers often find themselves in the unique position of neither belonging to the Latino culture with whom they work nor do they feel entirely a part of the dominant European-American communities from which they come. They could be considered what Giroux (1991) refers to as "border crossers," defined as teachers who are proficient in the languages and the practices of both cultural groups, who interact and negotiate between these cultures, and who adapt their behaviors in accord with each cultural context. To what extent, however, do they participate in a border pedagogy that challenges them to rethink how "the relations between dominant and subordinate groups are organized, how they are implicated and often structured in dominance, and how such relations might be transformed in order to promote a democratic and just society" (Giroux, 1991, p. 10)? Without sharing the home culture of the students they teach, how successful are bilingual, European-American teachers once they are practicing in the classroom?

In these times of controversy and uncertainty surrounding the education of language-minority students, teachers are faced with enormous challenges. Policy decisions over what is best for English language learners are often polarized around misconceptions, stereotypes, and political agendas of those governing bodies that are in positions of power. Families who are poor or do not speak English, and who are most affected by these decisions, have little representation, while their teachers are caught in the middle with the responsibility for the education of all students in their classrooms.

It is in this light that I bring to surface the voices of Euro-American bilingual teachers, whose perspectives are relevant in the ongoing struggle for education that is transformative and socially just. The experiences of these teachers reflect a growing awareness and understanding of their identity and role in a bicultural context, and will become more relevant with the increasing number of mainstream White teachers who are and will be working with English language learners in their classrooms. From the many recorded dialogues, written reflections, and informal discussions, I will share the highlights of research that has revealed multiple, complex issues regarding their teaching practice.

Claiming Our Euro-American Identity

I do not make an effort to identify myself ethnically, I make an effort not *to.—TERRI*

In our first group dialogues, we grappled with the task of identifying oneself as an ethnic person. This became problematic when, as each of us "tried on" different identifiers, we felt more or less uncomfortable with each. Many Euro-Americans resist seeing themselves as ethnic poeple or persons of racial identity, claiming that they "don't see color." This phenomenon of White ethnic unconsciousness has been named by many of the previously mentioned scholars of multicultural education as a symptom of White racism, which only serves to obscure the inequitable power relations between dominant and subordinate groups whose identities are defined and maintained by those in power around the very same racial constructs that they refuse to see. *White* is a term that is common when defining the Euro-American as having a racial identity among people of color, although this creates strong negative reactions among many Euro-Americans who do not wish to claim themselves as "White."

Class differences and social status among groups of Euro-Americans must also be acknowledged, as well as ethnic heritage, for the diversity of this group cannot simply be reduced to one homogenous culture. Nick, who rejects the identification with "American," points to his socioeconomic status, ethnic, and religious background as a part of his culture. The desire to know more about his "roots" is overpowering. His interpretation reveals a political awareness of an "America" that is oppressive:

What I perceive as "American" is not me. I do not feel that there is "liberty and justice for all," and I often feel part of an

*oppressor group; guilt by association. I can say that I am
proud to be part of a blue collar-middle class family. This is
more of an identification of a socioeconomic class than a "culture." I feel being raised as a Catholic is definitely part of who
I am, despite the fact that I am no longer a member of that
Church. But it did give me values that I think helped me
develop my social consciousness. I am one-half German, one-
fourth Polish, and one-fourth French Canadian (Quebecois).
I have no real connection, nor strong memories, really from
these cultures. . . . I think that definitely there is a part of me
that craves "roots."*

Elise, in her very direct and straightforward manner, said in the
first dialogue, "I never tell anybody I'm from America, because it
just grates on me, like chalk on a blackboard." She later wrote:

*My culture is a more or less even mix of German and English.
I see value in my culture. I like what I feel are hard working,
German values and I really like the English prose and poetry.
I feel my second culture (Hispanic) also has a great value and
I particularly like the emphasis on family and not taking life
so seriously.*

In coming to terms with claiming an ethnic identity, I have
found the work of Nieto (1992) most helpful in this discussion. She
describes a terminology that responds to two criteria: (1) What do
people want to be called? and (2) What is the most precise term?
The group of teachers who were the focus of this project represents those people whose roots are from Western European countries, and whose families, over generations, have been completely
assimilated into the English-speaking society in the United States,
as described in the work of Alba (1990). All of the participants
agreed that they did not like to associate with what they individually perceived as *American,* a term that I do not favor, as it implies
that Euro-Americans are the norm by which all other Americans
are measured. Therefore, we decided that the term *European-American* or *Euro-American* was acceptable because it attempts to be

accurate. The terms *White* and *Anglo* were also used among us, in varying contexts, which is later discussed.

Finding Common Ground

After the first meeting, the teachers had developed a sense of ownership and purpose, which are key to the participatory process. As each related how he or she came into teaching in bilingual classrooms, we discovered our common experiences, which established a fundamental framework from which we could later construct a more critical view of the realities of our work. Although we had entered the field at different times in our careers and through different avenues into various educational settings, those experiences and desires that led us towards working with Spanish-speaking students surfaced as (1) Spanish language acquisition and cross-cultural experiences, (2) feeling compelled to remedy the oppressive conditions for Spanish-speaking students, and (3) appreciation and making a difference.

Ryan, Nick, Nancy Jean, and Jessica acquired Spanish proficiency before entering the bilingual classroom. For them, learning another language was an extension of their formal education and a way to open doors to jobs where they could use their bilingual skills. They had all spent extended periods of time during their younger adult years working and traveling in Spanish-speaking countries (Mexico, Central America, and South America) and in Spanish-speaking communities in the United States. Through their cross-cultural experiences, they reflected an awareness of their ability to establish meaningful connections with Spanish-speaking populations. Nick describes this aspect of making connections:

> *The fact that I was fluent in Spanish got me a job as a program coordinator for "Mi Cultura," a grass-roots daycare after-school program in the Chicano barrio in St. Paul, Minnesota. I was able to become close friends with some people in that community and was able to participate quite intimately in some of their lives. My ability to speak Spanish and my*

concern for social justice and working with oppressed groups led to several teaching positions in experimental schools in the early 70s.

In addition to facilitating connections to Spanish-speaking communities, these four participants expressed that learning languages was one of their strengths. As Ryan added, "I loved Spanish class and absorbed the language like a maniac."

Elise, Valerie, and Terri were already experienced teachers when they saw the need to develop proficiency in Spanish. They moved into bilingual positions while simultaneously studying their second language and teaching Spanish-speaking children. As adult learners of a second language, this has been a longer, more arduous process for them. Both Terri and Elise went through enormous efforts to pass the California Bilingual Certificate of Competence (BCC), a requirement for teaching in bilingual classrooms. Terri survived her first year in a bilingual classroom by "writing a script each night for the following day and by having the kindest, most helpful (bilingual) teaching assistant one could wish for."

Wanting to remedy oppressive conditions was another common purpose that we identified. Each of us expressed a strong response to what we perceived was unjust in education, especially for students who were learning English. Elise's reasons were: "I became a bilingual teacher after 15 years in my district because I wanted to help Spanish-speaking children." Terri, who started in education as a preschool teacher, had another view on this theme:

When my children were 2 and 3 years old, I took them to the local nursery school in Ocean Park where we lived. The program was a "pressure-cooker" approach, funded by the federal government. The population was mostly Hispanic. I felt the oppression of the women, and wished to help them. I felt the inappropriateness of the approach: English only, teacher directed.

Also evident in the discussion of becoming a bilingual teacher was the sense of appreciation for their work by students and their parents. Valerie, who reentered teaching as a substitute teacher after having raised four children, quickly became aware of the rewards of working with English language learners:

> *While I was subbing one day, I was asked to take an ESL teacher's classes for the day. The assignment they had was very boring and I decided to make it fun. When I finished, the students really showed their appreciation. I was shocked and overwhelmed by their display of gratitude. So I looked into teaching ESL and found a class starting that weekend at a nearby college. I decided that teaching English to students who really wanted to learn was a real treat.*

Jessica, discussing her first experiences in student teaching in Chicago explained:

> *That area had a large number of new Mexican immigrants who came to work in the factories. Most of the Mexicans in the community were recent arrivals and were grateful to anyone who could be a bridge between them and the mainstream culture.*

These sentiments continued to surface through the ongoing dialogues and reflections with the participants.

Critically Viewing and "Problematizing" Our Experiences

As mentioned earlier, acknowledging ourselves as *Euro* or *White* Americans and claiming an ethnic identity was our first step toward defining ourselves as subjects in this project. Through this process, we were able to discover that a part of our struggle was about self-acceptance. This underscored another concern experienced by all, and that was the knowledge that we may never be entirely accepted into the Latino cultures with whom we worked. We realized that even though we have access to two cultures, we could not necessarily claim to be bicultural, or could we?

This situation was not only due to differences in language and culture, which Euro-American bilingual teachers have worked tremendously hard to overcome, but also because we could not change our *Whiteness.* Teachers shared that they were often the object of anger and resentment or that there were invisible barriers between them and their Latino colleagues. This caused them to feel excluded and sometimes inappropriate in their positions. Nick wrote in his reflections, "Sometimes I simply feel that I was born the wrong color." Terri explained this sentiment in more detail:

> *I have felt that. Not that I was born the wrong color, but there isn't anything I can do about it and I wish I could have. I wish I could have chosen a different skin so I could be more effective in what I do. Because what I do is with this community, and when I felt desperate about being where I am, and wanting to be anywhere else, I couldn't be somewhere else because* this *is what I do. And if I left, I would have to go to a White community. And I didn't want to do that, because this is what I like doing, this is what I do best, this is what I busted my butt to learn how to do ... and I want to do it, and I feel rewarded doing it, but I also feel limited by the skin that I'm in.*

Elise wrote in her reflections that she could probably be more bicultural if she "looked" and "acted" more Mexican, and this would help her be more accepted.

We began to understand that even though White teachers can learn the language and become more culturally literate in their interactions with the Latino communities in which they work, they can never really share the same lived experiences as those who are subordinated by the dominant White culture. Being a Euro-American in the United States implies a history of privilege that sets one apart from people of color in ways that can never be ignored; this was the most difficult issue to accept. As much as we desire to join oppressed people in their struggles, we cannot change who we are in this process.

Acceptance, however, can happen over time, as explained by Nick, when trust is established between people through our actions. In his case, a simple handshake meant so much to him:

I helped out one time for a Mother's Day "Día de la Madre" presentation. I stayed more than I had to stay and I did more than I had to do, and at the end, one of the guys just shook my hand and gave me the handshake. As simple as it was, I felt really good about that.... Throughout the year I began to feel that just because I was an "Anglo," I wasn't an infiltrator from the administration; that I was taking stands with them, and I was defending their positions, and I wasn't betraying them. By the end of the year I was starting to feel, and I'm hoping that by the beginning of next year they may say, "OK, this guy is all right. We can trust him, and he'll stand with us."

Ryan described more openly the kind of acceptance that acknowledges that Euro-Americans are not always ignorant of other cultures and that they, too, can participate in meaningful discussions about Latino communities:

I don't want to be accepted as another Latino, because I'm not, and I never will be. So I think I'm looking for a kind of acceptance that comes out of respect for what I know and what I can do. Sometimes I get a sense, for example, from my Chicano colleagues, that Mexico is their country and it is their own, and that if I know something about it, it's not really valid—that my experience in Latin America is not really as valid as their experience in Latin America. And I do have this experience that is really just as valid as theirs.

The need to continue developing proficiency in Spanish language and cultural awareness was also highlighted in our work together. Although most of the participants felt comfortable and natural using Spanish most of the time, they also became painfully aware that they had limitations in Spanish as their second language. This was especially true when dealing with the familiar, informal, and more affective uses of language. Most expressed a frustration, awkwardness, and often embarrassment, as Jessica described her experiences being immersed in a different culture:

*It's like playing a game where everyone knows the rules but
you, and when you've broken a rule, it's like hitting an invisible wall. The only way you know is from people's responses.
The rules seem to be an unspoken code, which is innately
understood by everyone who has been raised in the culture.
You hear the words and understand the words but don't know
the context in which they are spoken.*

Nick described his inability, at times, to use and understand the
common expressions, jokes, and idioms shared among members of a
culture in which he already feels like an outsider:

*Even when I do hear rhymes in Spanish, sometimes I have a
difficult time; my ear is not attuned to them properly. Sometimes they go too fast, or sometimes they're nonsense kinds of
things, like "Hickory, dickory dock, the mouse ran up the
clock"; if you were trying to understand that, you would say,
"What the hell are they talking about? What's so special about
that?" and the same thing happens in Spanish, and I don't
know what makes it good or what.*

He explained how this affects his confidence level when working
with Spanish-speaking parents in the literacy classes he teaches:
"It's just not having the cultural experience of growing up there, . . . I
don't have enough confidence. I mean my Spanish is good, but I
don't have the finesse with it."

Valerie's experience with language and her actions to understand it were also shared. In her high school ESL classes she realized that there was some "inappropriate" language being used by
the students:

*I could tell by the looks on the girls faces that the boys were
using some offensive language. And I couldn't catch it. My
ear wasn't tuned finely enough. Even though the teacher aide
would repeat what they were saying, and she tried to teach me
a few words, the students talked so fast and they mumbled,
that I couldn't catch it. So that next summer, I went to Cuer-*

navaca, and I paid one of the tutors four hours of tutoring time to teach me all the foul language in Spanish. Then I walked into the classroom in September, and the first time some kid said "chinga" (synonym for the "F" word), out the door! And he looked at me, like, "How did she know that?"

Valerie went on to say that, as she needed to learn the codes of language within their cultural context, she also felt that it was her responsibility to teach students who are new to this country the codes of appropriate behavior in classrooms in the United States.

The politics surrounding language and teaching in schools was also examined and challenged throughout the project. The participants claimed that efforts to maintain programs that support teaching and learning in two languages are often challenged by forces that perpetuate transmissive, authoritative approaches to teaching. As perceived by Elise, these latter approaches become the method by which students who speak another language are "molded" to fit into the dominant society, and are encouraged to get rid of their native tongue:

And if you want somebody to lose the culture, because you don't like the culture, and you want them to be whatever Americans are supposed to be, then the best thing you can do is take their language away from them first. Because that's going to start taking everything else away.

A significant question arose at this point: What is the goal of an educational system that teaches literacy skills in a second language to English speakers as a "foreign" language, and that does not teach these skills to students who already speak these languages? Those who come to our schools speaking Spanish too often have not had opportunities to develop their native language skills. These individuals, who would be best equipped to become future bilingual teachers, often cannot read and write in the language they first learned as a child.

On the other hand, the Euro-American bilingual teachers who may have formal language training are more likely to be lacking in cross-cultural experience, which, from their perspective, defines a clear boundary between them and the culture in which they are seeking acceptance. We clearly saw the need for a higher representation of native Spanish speakers in classrooms as teachers. This did not mean that we perceived a Euro-American bilingual teacher as unsuitable for these students. On the contrary; we saw ourselves as uniquely equipped to work with language-minority children, for we have also experienced the process of acquiring a second language and have also felt the pain of being "out of place" and different. Having lived similar experiences has contributed a more sensitive approach to the needs of these students.

We collectively experienced that bilingual educators have to deal with what we referred to as a "monolingual ignorance" about language learning and a viewpoint that is reactive to languages other than English. Elise challenged this view, "Students are seen with their language as a disease. They say these students *only* speak Spanish. Well, what about *only* speaking English? Isn't that a disease, too?" It was the consensus of all that bilingualism needs to be fostered by all teachers and that we must continuously encourage biliteracy in the classroom setting and within the school community not only for the language minority but for the language majority as well.

Issues surrounding the dominant paradigm in schools were eventually revealed in our discussions and challenged—not only as pertaining to perceptions of language but also in our teacher behaviors. Ryan expressed:

> *I tend to fall back on patterns of dominance over my students. I really hate it when I get bogged down in dealing with student misbehavior in negative ways like scolding and punishing and embarrassing students.... It is how I remember teachers dealing with me.... I try to overcome this by remembering caring teachers and imagining what they would do in a similar situation.*

Terri shared that she had to learn to resist the temptation to "lift up the little chin of the child to look the teacher in the eye." Most of us in the dominant culture seek eye contact, yet in many other cultures it is considered a sign of disrespect to look an adult in the eye.

Dominant Eurocentric patterns are also interwoven into curriculum and in a pervasive view that children whose language is not English are remedial and do not belong in the higher-level classes. At Ryan's school, he struggled with getting students into the "International Baccalaureate" program, in which students could take advanced placement. Jessica stated, "I feel that at my school . . . the bilingual kids are 'my problem'; ESL is 'my thing'" and Elise was frustrated over not having equity in the resources for her students:

> *We need to convince other teachers that bilingual students deserve an equal share of the pie (i.e., same amount of materials). Bilingual teachers shouldn't have to always be translating language, books, ideas, etc., into Spanish. We have a clerk who interferes a lot and puts up obstacles in the way of bilingual teachers. She orders materials and has much more influence than she should.*

We found that all of us had moved through these obstacles by creating innovative programs and networking with other colleagues who were willing to collaborate and share in improving programs for their Spanish-speaking students. Elise was able to organize with her colleagues to create a lending library and book-sharing program called "Club Literario," which also brought many of her parents to school.

Ryan identified several key elements that created an environment in which his students could succeed:

Staying in touch with the families
Allowing students to choose the language they use in science class (and other content classes)
Using "hands-on" projects
Creating a collaborative/cooperative group environment
Having high expectations
Maintaining a classroom library of books in Spanish
Reading stories in Spanish

Having the principal visit the room to see projects
Writing in journals
Making books

His Spanish literacy class even became a part of the daily student body announcements, by announcing in Spanish what had traditionally been done only in English. According to Ryan, "The International Baccalaureate program set the stage. They would just take the P.A. system whenever they felt like it." So Ryan saw no reason why his students could not do the same:

People complained about the Spanish announcements, especially the bilingual teachers. They thought the Spanish-speaking kids should hear the announcements in English so they could learn more English. I told the teachers that if the Spanish-speaking kids could understand more school activities, they would feel more welcome and may participate more. The Spanish literacy class that worked on the announcements was very resistant to learning before we took on that project. I had to defend the rationale for the project at a faculty meeting. I presented petitions that the students had written and circulated, calling for continuing the morning announcements in Spanish. They had collected more than 250 signatures in 24 hours. The principal (a Chicana) was uncomfortable with the project at first; now she is really supportive.

Ryan added why he saw this as such an important way to advocate for students, as they saw him as someone who would "go to bat" for them. "I think this is something an Anglo teacher can do for the school and for the kids."

In addition, we all realized that the administrators at the schools play a key role in advocating in favor of these students. Valerie's story about support is interesting:

In September, . . . I placed eight students in geometry. Most of them came to me within a few days and said they could not understand the teacher. The head counselor let me shop around and find a teacher who would speak more slowly. One of the teachers I spoke to became angry and defensive when I told him that he spoke too rapidly to be understood by my recently mainstreamed students.

None of the teachers were interested in learning SDAIE (Specially Designed Academic Instruction in English) methods, and saw themselves not as a part of a whole learning process, but as a separate life in the world of mathematics. So a battle raged for the rest of the school year because a fellow LEP [limited-English proficient] science teacher and I wanted a laboratory science taught in SDAIE or Spanish, plus I wanted a sheltered geometry class. We finally had to drop our insistence on both and unite to fight for a lab science, biology, to be taught as a LEP course.

What . . . we faced was ignorance on the part of the administrators, even the principal who had wanted the PEP [Power English Program] program in the first place said, "What are they going to do with biology?" and "Why can't they learn English first?"

Finally, the assistant superintendent came to the school, pointed out that there were enough students signed up, 38, that there was an interested and available teacher, and that state guidelines and district policy all dictated that the LEP student be given full access to the curriculum.

Constructing a Critical Knowledge Base for Transforming Practices

The need for these teachers to share their experiences was articulated in all of our dialogues, and by critically examining these experiences, we were discovering problematic issues that were shaping the nature of our work. Through this in-depth analysis of our shared experiences, we were able to define the following concerns, or themes, which constructed a critical knowledge base for emancipatory action:

- The need for gaining acceptance, by others and within ourselves
- The need to continue developing proficiency in Spanish language and cultural awareness
- The need to question the dominant paradigms found in traditional practices and improve our teaching practice through innovative and organic approaches
- The need to make meaningful connections within the (Latino) communities in which we work

Critical pedagogy can provide a framework for educators to see themselves and their students in a more dynamic and meaningful relationship. By reflecting on their actions, learning to question and to listen, a new understanding of knowledge and how it is created can begin to form. Through a genuine interaction and negotiation of knowledge with their students, as opposed to the transmission of knowledge to their students, teachers and students can develop a voice and become more open to each other and transformed as mutual learners in the classroom (Freire, 1986).

A critical approach is needed in order for teachers to become more authentic with their students as well as interpret the world in which they operate as professionals, to question their own actions or inactions, and to deliberate on how to bring about change.

The participants spoke specifically to the actions they would like to see occur in their schools, among their co-workers, and also actions on the study itself. Some of the recommendations for action are self-fulfilling as a result of personal transformation, others are a direct message to others to listen to their message. For most of the participants, this study has opened up a dialogue that they would like to see continued, in one form or another.

From the beginning, Elise stated that it was important to continue meeting and to bring this dialogue to the attention of administrators and fellow teachers:

This shouldn't be the end; we're starting this as a nucleus, maybe as a way to give support, so we don't feel as if we're divided and separated.... We've got people to talk to that understand where we're coming from and what our thoughts are and what's happening.

The Potential Roles as Border Crossers and Bridge Builders

Quoting Ryan:

> *I perceive my role to be to learn about the language and culture of my students and to learn about my students' communities and families; to learn to see and understand racism and the role of White people in perpetuating it. To learn to see the effects of racism on our students and to learn to fight racism in the system and within myself. I need to be a role model for other Whites and be a change agent. To overcome racism, one needs to work toward empowering individuals who belong to oppressed groups.*

The Euro-American teacher's reflections on issues of culture, power, and pedagogy in their daily realities brought to surface the necessary actions that they were already considering and would need to take after the conclusion of this study. The process of generating themes for dialogue, discovering new knowledge, and, most importantly, recognizing those practices that were collectively changing the realities for themselves and their students constituted the potential actions the participants felt were necessary for creating meaningful praxis in their roles as Euro-American bilingual educators.

We discovered our roles and potentials as "border crossers" being fulfilled in the following actions:

1. Serving as a bridge between the Spanish- and English-speaking communities through cultural work in both communities:

   - Increasing awareness and sensitivity among school staff of other cultural perspectives
   - Investigating the issues of inequity surrounding language and literacy that are caused by hegemonic structures in schools
   - Acknowledging both formal language and the language used in the community as valid for vehicles in preserving and valuing cultural diversity

- Using one's cross-cultural experiences as an asset to establish meaningful connections with the communities

2. Challenging the structures that perpetuate transmissive, authoritarian, and ethnocentric approaches to teaching

   - Advocating for Spanish-speaking students' access to core and enrichment programs where they can achieve high levels of academic performance and dispel the stigma of "remedial" and "deficit" that are too often associated with bilingual education
   - Educating their monolingual peers on second-language acquisition
   - Reflecting on one's own practices in the classroom and how they may either perpetuate inequitable structures or contribute to changing those inequities, thereby empowering students
   - Rethinking one's own ethnic "baggage"
   - Breaking down barriers through open dialogue and learning from each other through a willingness to surrender power
   - Working from an established base of support to create changes within the system
   - Understanding the school principal as a key agent in gaining support and influencing programs for students
   - Networking with other educators who share common goals to collectively achieve change
   - Using innovative approaches to move around bureaucratic obstacles that may exist, such as lack of funding

Conclusion

The most significant implications of this study are realized when considering the continuing need to improve the nation's teacher education programs to better train excellent bilingual, cross-culturally aware teachers who are prepared to take on the challenges of working in diversity. This study makes specific recommendations for teacher education programs, such as including coursework on

"White Heritage" in multicultural classrooms, teaching critical pedagogy, and offering opportunities for continued language and cross-cultural awareness development—not only for future bilingual teachers but also for monolingual teachers who will be working with language-minority students.

The findings of this study also have major implications for current practices within existing bilingual programs. The issues of program support and support for the needs particular to Euro-American bilingual teachers, as strongly articulated by the participants in the study, must be attended to in order for bilingual education to be successful. In particular, the needs of the Euro-American bilingual teacher are very different from the needs of the Latino bilingual educator. Just as students in our classrooms must be provided with appropriate instruction, teachers in bilingual programs must be given opportunities for growth that are appropriate for their linguistic and cultural backgrounds.

Having access to two cultures, the Euro-American educator who becomes a border crosser has a responsibility. The knowledge one holds from both worlds is very valuable, not only to those who they serve from the Latino community but also to their own community of Euro-Americans.

It is the responsibility for the Euro-American teachers to become the cultural workers whose job is to break down the stereotypes, illusions, and misunderstandings that exist between people of different languages. Through their actions in schools and through critical dialogue among their peers, their students, and their communities, the goals of mutual understanding and respect for each other may be attained. This kind of work is very necessary if the nation wants to build alliances for a more harmonious world. Choice is power. People can choose to cross borders or they can return to their comfortable worlds of privilege and not participate in their second culture.

The participants shared that progress in their work has come out of several hard-earned lessons about who they were as White teachers, what their strengths were, and where their limitations existed. They realized that their work was infinitely more challenging than that of English-only teaching, and that they were often not appreciated or understood. They would always have to be engaged in political controversy and always need to fight for and defend their programs. Their experiences have demanded that they continuously improve and reexamine their motives for teaching in bilingual classrooms.

The daily realities and experiences that enabled each to see his or her own dominant culture also prompted the surfacing of a better understanding of racism, classism, and privilege that was prevalent within our own upbringings. For the Euro-American educator to see the invisible power associated with being White and English speaking is an ongoing, introspective process from which we can all learn.

It is critical that people do not see this kind of work as only belonging to bilingual teachers. As discovered in many follow-up dialogues and in conferences that included a larger audience, it has been strongly noted that a monolingual teacher can also make a positive and critical contribution by caring and incorporating a mulitcultural perspective in his or her daily teaching and toward the larger efforts of school reform.

References

Ada, A. F. (1990). *A magical encounter: Spanish language children's literature in the classroom*. Compton, CA: Santillana.

Alba, R. (1990). *Ethnic identity: The transformation of white America*. New Haven, CT: Yale University Press.

Banks, J. A. (1995). Multicultural education: Historical development, dimensions, and practice. In J. A. Banks & C. A. M. Banks (Eds.), *Handbook of research on multicultural education*. New York: Simon & Schuster.

Canales, J. (1992). A pedagogical framework for bilingual education teacher preparation programs. In *Proceedings of the Third National Research Symposium on Limited English Proficient Student Issues: Focus on Middle and High School Issues* (pp. 113–154). Washington, DC: National Clearinghouse for Bilingual Education.

Chisholm, I. M. (1994, Winter). Preparing teachers for multicultural classrooms. *The Journal of Educational Issues of Language Minority Students 14,* pp. 43–67.

Cummins, J. (1989). *Empowering minority students.* Sacramento: California Association for Bilingual Education.

Darder, A. (1993). *Culture and power in the classroom: A critical foundation for bilingual education.* New York: Bergin & Garvey.

Darder, A., & Upshur, C. (1992). *What do Latino children need to succeed in school? A study of four Boston public schools.* (Doc. 92-02 No. ED344951). Mauricio Gaston Institute, University of Massachusetts at Boston.

Delpit, L. (1995). *Other people's children: Cultural conflict in the classroom.* New York: New Press.

EdSource. (1998). *Election brief: Proposition 227, "English for the Children."* Palo Alto, CA: Author.

Fredrickson, J. (Ed.). (1995). *Reclaiming our voices: Bilingual education, critical pedagogy and praxis.* Ontario: California Association for Bilingual Education.

Freeman, D. E., & Freeman, Y. (1994). *Between worlds: Access to second language acquisition.* Portsmouth, NH: Heinemann.

Freire, P. (1970). *Pedagogy of the oppressed.* New York: Continuum.

Freire, P. (1986). *Education for critical consciousness.* New York: Continuum.

Freire, P. (1994). *Pedagogy of hope* (Robert R. Barr, Trans.). New York: Continuum.

Freire, P., & Macedo, D. (1987). *Literacy: Reading the word and the world.* South Hadley, MA: Bergin & Garvey.

Giroux, H. (1991). Democracy, border pedagogy and the politics of difference. In *Seminar on critical pedagogy* (pp. 1–33), unpublished manuscript, University of San Francisco.

Hidalgo, N. M. (1993). Multicultural teacher introspection. In L. Perry & J. Fraser (Eds.), *Freedom's plow: Teaching in the multicultural classroom* (pp. 99–106). New York: Routledge.

hooks, b. (1994). *Teaching to transgress.* New York: Routledge.

Krashen, S., & Biber, D. (1988). *On course: Bilingual education's success in California.* Sacramento: California Association for Bilingual Education.

Laughlin, M. C. (1996). *Crossing borders: Transformative experiences of Euro American bilingual teachers in a Spanish speaking context. A participatory study.* Unpublished doctoral dissertation, University of San Francisco.

McIntosh, P. (1988). *White privilege and male privilege: A personal account of coming to see correspondences through work in women's studies.*

(Working Paper No. 189). Wellesley, MA: Wellesley College Center for Research on Women.

Mcyntire, A. (1997). *Making meaning of whiteness: Exploring racial identity with white teachers*. Albany: State University of New York Press.

Nieto, S. (1992). *Affirming diversity: The sociopolitical context of multicultural education* (2nd ed.). White Plains, NY: Longman.

Paley, V. (1979). *White teacher*. Cambridge, MA: Harvard University Press.

Quintanar-Sarellana, R. (1991). *Teacher's perception of the language and culture of linguistic minority students*. Unpublished doctoral dissertation, Stanford University.

Scarcella, R. (1990). *Teaching language minority students in the multicultural classroom*. Englewood Cliffs, NJ: Prentice-Hall.

Shor, I., & Freire, P. (1987). *A pedagogy for liberation: Dialogues on transforming education*. New York: Bergin & Garvey.

Sleeter, C., & McClaren, P. (Eds.). (1995). *Multicultural education, critical pedagogy, and the politics of difference*. Albany: State University of New York Press.

Tinajero, J. V., & Ada, A. F. (Ed.). (1992). *The power of two languages: Literacy and biliteracy for Spanish speaking students*. New York: Macmillan/McGraw-Hill.

12

The Teacher in a Critical Leadership Role

JOSÉ A. LÓPEZ

> *Although social justice is fueled by philosophical and academic discussions, it is the daily events and conversations of school life that carry the weight of the struggle for good schooling. Sometimes they sway a school, sometimes they move a class, and sometimes they change the world one student at a time.*—OAKES & LIPTON (1999)

There is an abundance of evidence on the need for leadership for successful school reform. Much of the literature most often views leadership as a direct action of administrators, the formal leaders of schools. We are now learning of the value of teachers as leaders for school change. Teacher leadership is an essential ingredient for the integration of multicultural education in schools.

When viewed from a transformative or constructivist perspective, a much broader view of leadership can be seen. I define *leadership* as a set of processes that enable the participants to construct individual meanings about the issues and use those understandings to develop a sense of common purpose. These processes engage all citizens of the school's communities (López, 1996). In addition, two other definitions of leaders and teacher leaders form the framework for this chapter. Lambert and colleagues (1996, p. 99) define a *teacher leader* as "one who creates an environment in which participants are encouraged to make their own meaning from their own experiences." Rallis (1989, p. 201) describes a *leader* as a "catalyst, guide, interpreter, and facilitator for a process." In this view, the most important roles of formal school leaders are as follows:

1. Foster teacher leadership by cultivating in teachers the belief that they play an important role in school reform. Administrators can influence this by supporting teachers in trying new and different ideas in their classrooms and in schoolwide activities. They actively encourage teachers to experiment without suffering consequences if new ideas do not work as planned. These actions will help establish trust in the formal leadership by the teachers.

2. Create opportunities for teachers to assume leadership roles. An extension of fostering leadership is providing ways in which teachers can assume responsibilities outside their classrooms. Administrators who value teacher leadership will include teachers in major decisions affecting the school. These could be programmatic, where teachers either directly decide on programs to be implemented or advise the administrator on the advantages or disadvantages of different programs. There are many other areas where administrators can create leadership opportunities for teachers. Some of these include:

   • Personal selection (admisnistrators, teachers, and staff)
   • Staff development (content and scheduling)
   • Student assessment procedures
   • Budgetary decisions (budget development and allotment of funds)
   • Curriculum (selection and revision)
   • Parental involvement

3. Develop leadership within the school faculty and community. Formal schoolwide decision-making structures legitimatize the

role of teacher leaders in the school. Structures such as Leadership Teams, School Site Councils, Principal's Cabinets, and ad hoc groups exercise formal leadership that is shared with the administrators of the school. Not only are the voices of teachers valued, but in major decisions, teachers' voices are equal to that of administrators. Administrators who understand the strength of true shared decision making delegate responsibility and authority to make decisions.

To foster, create, and develop leadership does require preparation. These actions by administrators call for a change in the traditional roles and relationships between teachers and the school's formal leadership. Many administrators are not trained in the concept of *teacher leadership* and will also need additional preparation.

This vision of leadership is the foundation used to identify important teacher leadership knowledge, competencies, and skills for multicultural education in schools.

Values, Beliefs, and Purpose: The Starting Points for Leadership

Between stimulus and response, between the open delicate leaves of the sensitive plant and its closing in response to touch, is the unique (maybe other creatures can do this too, and I am being a humanist!) human ability to choose through self-awareness, imagination, conscience, or independent will to do something different. The choice is between being a victim or being proactive. This is not a facile, simple task and I do not mean to imply that it is. When I work with students on the "isms," I stress awareness and action, not blame. Look at the stimulus. What will you choose to do about it?
—*HIGH SCHOOL TEACHER, ALAMEDA, CA*

The term *critical multicultural education* brings to mind many different interpretations by teachers, parents, and administrators alike. The starting point of leadership for major reform initiatives is the creation of opportunities, processes, and structures for school staffs and communities to explore, discuss, and identify common values, beliefs, and meanings. Too often, schools either ignore this important phase in the change process or they shortchange it by not providing enough time to hear all points of view and to reach consensus. The role of teacher leaders is critical in this process because of the level of influence and trust that teachers have with parents, students, colleagues, and administrators. In culturally diverse communities, parents view teachers with much respect and greatly value their opinions regarding their children's schooling.

Fullan (1991, 1993), Hargraves (1997), Evans (1996), and other researchers on the educational change process point to the need for teachers to "buy in" to the innovation or accept it as valid and necessary. Some teachers will resist change either overtly or covertly if they are not involved in some significant way in creating it. Meaningful involvement means when teachers are given opportunities to do the following:

- Determine the need for change by examining the current situation.
- Create meaning and determine the intent or purpose of possible changes.
- Explore alternatives to improve the current situation.
- Discuss the impacts that alternatives will have on their teaching and students.
- Have input on the decision to accept an alternative.
- Receive necessary professional development.
- Evaluate the effectiveness of the change on their teaching and students.

Role of Teacher Leaders in Exploring Values, Beliefs, and Purpose

Teacher leaders play an important part in influencing the discussions that create change toward a multicultural vision of schools. There are several factors to consider:

1. Use informal methods, such as:

   - Observations of meetings (i.e., faculty, parent groups, etc.)
   - Noticing formal and informal interactions between and among teachers, students, parents, staff, and administrators
   - Listening to informal teacher talk to gather "insider" view of how the school's adults value diversity

This view is how teachers, students, administrators, and parents understand, deal with, react to, and feel about multicultural education. This is invaluable in determining the issues that may arise in this change effort.

2. On a more formal basis, review and assess data, including:

   - Achievement (standardized tests results, grade-point averages, drop-out rates, graduation rates, district-mandated curriculum aligned tests, passing and failure rates, etc.)
   - Disciplinary actions (suspensions, office referrals, expulsions, in-school suspensions, detentions, etc.)
   - Attendance (attendance rates, attendance by classes and/or teachers, reasons for absences, etc.)
   - Class enrollment ("special needs" classes, such as Advanced Placement, college preparatory, special education, gifted and talented, remedial, bilingual education, ESL, etc.)
   - Parental involvement (some schools keep data on certain types of parental involvement, such as teacher contacts, conferences, membership in parent organizations, etc.)

Information gathered by whatever method is valuable in determining how much support or resistance can be expected in creating an active, visible respect and value for diversity and implementing multicultural education.

Support from Colleagues

Cultivate support from individuals whose actions and behaviors show respect and value change. The teacher leaders should initiate conversations with a goal to create movement toward bringing about a dialogue with the larger faculty and community. This also fosters the further development of teacher leadership. In sharing your views with others, different perspectives may arise that provide more information for the assessment of current conditions.

Exploring Beliefs and Values Toward Diversity and Critical Multicultural Education

Adults as well as children must create meaning and purpose in major change initiatives. This does not occur until one examines one's internal beliefs and values. Discussions about race, culture, and diversity are often difficult in any organization. Schools are not different. When teacher leaders lead and engage in such conversations and dialogue, they can challenge, affirm, and show respect for diverse perspectives.

The goal of such activities should be to allow teachers and administrators to examine and assess one's values and beliefs. Transformative teaching and learning practices reach the critical moment at this point, beginning the leadership process for change.

Building Connections

When the district and schools' monthly schedules proclaim February as Black History month, May as Hispanic Heritage, and talk about Asian contributions in a specific week, something is definitely not right! Teaching about sensitivity, culture, discrimination, prejudice, contribution, and subjects of that nature, cannot have a rigid time-frame. They are either naturally and continuously part of our curriculum or they will become mandates, mandates that will not bring us closer and will be futile.
—*ELEMENTARY TEACHER LEADER, NEWARK, CA*

Effective teacher leadership is collaborative and shared among others. Traditional forms of top-down leadership is seen when administrators issue mandates and directives to teachers. This has proven to be ineffective and generally has the direct opposite effect to the acceptance and implementation of new ideas or programs. Teachers respond best to change when they have some control. Adults (and children) learn when they can connect the "new" to something with which they are familiar.

Major changes in schools have multidimensional effects, and often we are unaware of these impacts. The old saying that "two (or more) heads are better than one" could not be more true than in the leadership of today's schools. Fostering support is an important aspect of leadership. This does not mean, however, finding a majority of individuals that agree with your position. Fostering support means building connections with both formal and informal school leaders.

This process should be well-planned to anticipate potential issues and resistance that may arise. A collaborative planning approach increases the possibilities that a wide range of potential issues will surface. True collaboration means engaging significant and influential individuals in meaningful conversations about the school's performance and improvement. The goal is for the schools' communities to collectively identify the problems and determine possible alternative solutions. Attempts to determine these issues are most often a group process but at times it can be a highly personal approach, such as one-to-one conversations with significant and influential individuals in the school and community.

The Role of Teacher Leaders in Building Connections

There are several factors for teacher leaders to consider in building connections for the support of critical theory in multicultural education and other major school reform efforts:

- *Administrative Support:* Teacher leaders discuss their informal and formal assessments with the principal to secure support. The administrator also plays an important role in the school improvement process. Creating this connection provides valuable information as well as an opportunity to influence the beginning of the schoolwide discussion of values and beliefs. You may secure support and resources for this initial step or you may encounter resistance from the principal. In many cases, principals can effectively block, delay, or derail reform initiatives such as multicultural education. On the other hand, supportive principals can greatly enhance and influence successful implementation.

- *Collaborative Structures:* Many schools have shared decision-making structures, such as leadership teams, school advisory councils, grade-level committees, and academic teams or departments. If these groups are representative of the diverse voices of the faculty and community, the teacher leaders should participate and secure the support of these groups. Depending on the purpose of the collaborative groups, they may also assist or choose to direct the development of the process, structures, and other aspects of the plan.

- *Resistance:* Resistance to major changes, particularly an emotionally charged innovation such as multicultural education, is to be expected. Fullan (1993, p. 21) writes, "Problems are our friends." Undoubtedly, problems will arise but these should be seen as part of the change process. As in the initial assessment phase, teacher leaders should determine the diverse views of the group's members and be prepared to share their assessments and defend their positions. However, new perspectives may arise that have not been considered that should be included in any planning efforts. Fullan's (1991) work on change has led him to the conclusion about the failure of reform efforts. The main reason for failure is simple—developers or decision makers went through a process of acquiring their meaning of the new curriculum. But when it was presented to teachers, there was no provision for allowing them to work out the meaning of the changes for themselves (Fullan, 1991, p. 112).

Understanding the Process

Educational Change

> *I have a difficult time with change in my life. The fear of change strikes a chord with me. I am an advocate of reform no matter how big or small, however, in the back of my mind is the burning question, what will I lose? I experience that on a personal sense. On a professional level, I notice how change has lead to incredible tension. I am constantly working to urge our staff to use the new program, yet my efforts are met with angry resistance. I feel like the enemy. I feel like I am forcing something on the teachers that they desperately do not want to have any part of. But what do I do?*
>
> *—TEACHER / TECHNOLOGY SPECIALIST, SAN RAMON, CA*

One of the most important abilities any educational leader needs is understanding the process of change. As this teacher/technology specialist above illustrates, change is not easy. Even though the teacher leader has valuable knowledge and skills to share with her colleagues, she faced what seemed to her to be insurmountable struggles.

Why is change so difficult for teachers? Major change is hard for most people. However, there are many reasons why change is particularly difficult for educators. In this brief chapter, space permits only an outline of several important reasons. One reason is the history of schooling itself. The one-room schoolhouse placed teachers in individual rooms separate from their colleagues. Years of isolation led to limited communication about teaching and learning.

Change is also difficult for teachers because it can challenge their perceived competence. Most experienced teachers have a repertoire of strategies that work well for them. They also become knowledgeable of their content areas and with the texts and curriculum. Reforms such as multicultural education are often new for most teachers. Until recently, courses in multicultural education were not a normal part of teacher preparation programs. In many states, this is still not required of preservice programs.

One's attitude about the perceived change also impacts how it is received. Underlying values and beliefs about the need, importance, and desirability of multicultural education will undoubtedly affect how some educators accept it. As mentioned in the first section of this chapter, this is the starting point of leadership—it cannot be overlooked if successful implementation is to occur.

Change is a process and it takes time. Of all concerns that teachers have, the one I hear most often is the lack of time. I believe that this single factor can greatly hamper any innovation. Time is an integral part of most aspects of change:

- Learning and unlearning new and old assumptions
- Developing meaning and purpose
- Determining the need for the change
- Dealing with perceived incompetence with something new
- Training and professional development
- Practicing the new knowledge and skills in classrooms

A high school teacher leader describes the issue of time in her experience with the process of change as follows:

Change is a long process that takes time to accomplish. Teachers need that time to realize that change is necessary. Then it takes time to let go of old practices and to somehow connect them to new practices. Becoming comfortable with new practices takes training and time to integrate into the curriculum. It also takes personal time from trainers and leaders to help teachers through this stage. If teachers see themselves as being integral to the change planning and process, more effective change can take place.
—*HIGH SCHOOL ENGLISH TEACHER, VALLEJO, CA*

Role of Teacher Leaders in Facilitating the Process of Change

The first two sections of this chapter described how teacher leaders can begin the school improvement process. In facilitating the values, beliefs, and purposes as well as building connections, leaders are determining the need for multicultural education. I do not imply that these phases, once addressed, are completed by any means. The process described is a constant effort, always needing to be examined and reevaluated.

Educational leaders, teachers, and administrators must be aware of *what* happens during the change process and as well as *why* it happens. To describe this, I utilize Evans's (1996) framework, which he calls The Tasks of Change, as needed knowledge for leaders to learn. He describes the role of the leaders: "One must . . . help staff address the four dilemmas, help them move from loss to commitment, from old competence to new competence, from confusion to coherence, and from conflict to consensus" (p. 55).

Teacher leaders and administrators must understand each task and how persons making the change are feeling. Knowing these tasks can give different interpretation to certain behaviors in relation to implementing multicultural education.

1. *Resistance:* As mentioned earlier in this chapter, teachers will likely resist change if they feel they have had no voice or control in the decision-making process. The behavior of those tackling the first task of change (unfreezing) may appear to be resistance, but it may be fear or discomfort in letting go of the old, familiar, and comfortable before accepting the new. Leaders must listen to the concerns of these teachers and understand that it may not be possible to relieve their concerns. Most people making major changes such as multicultural education will experience some form of anxiety and discomfort. Understanding and listening to their concerns, and addressing them when possible, are the responsibility of the leaders.

2. *Lack of Meaning:* Some form of questioning or doubting from teachers may indicate that they have yet to acquire a full meaning of multicultural education. This task of moving from loss to commitment may be due to a lack of meaning rather than resistance to the innovation. However, Fullan (1991) found that clarity is not always possible before actual implementation. The meaning and purpose become clearer as teachers begin the inte-

gration of multicultural education into their teaching. As stated earlier, multicultural education is a complex concept. The implication is that the specifics that some teachers feel they need may not be possible to acquire before the actual start of the innovation. Support during the implementation then becomes an important job for leaders to assist teachers.

3. *Insufficient Skills or Knowledge:* New programs may require new behaviors as teachers move from their former competence to those required by the innovation. This is best achieved by well-planned professional development. Leaders must be aware of the most effective forms of making this available to teachers. Research on professional development should be reviewed and incorporated into the plan. Joyce and Showers (1995, p. 12) believe that the core of an effective professional development system is "the development of many small communities of teachers and administrators carefully linked within and across schools and supported by human and material resources." Much of their research points to some form of coaching as crucial in the implementation process. Joyce and Showers further describe a support cadre as "an essential component of an effective system is personnel who can offer instruction and support to others in the areas that are under study. These persons need to develop a very high level of competence in an area to the point where they can deal with its theory, demonstrate it, organize practice with it, and help coaching teams and study groups sustain its use in the instructional setting" (p. 15). The roles of leaders are to help create and sustain the system, and secure the necessary resources.

4. *Confusion:* Change can be confusing regardless of planning efforts. The impact that innovations have on teachers cannot always be anticipated. The preceding items address some common areas found by Evans (1996). Large-scale improvements may bring about a need for new or different structures. One such structure was the professional development system and the creation of a "support cadre" (mentioned earlier). The school staff, including administrators, and the community must understand the role and responsibilities of the new support team. What sup-

port can the members provide teachers? How does one access support from the team? What role does the principal play in the functioning of the team? How are decisions made and how are teachers involved in that process? The creation of any structure, its functions, and responsibilities must be clear to the faculty prior to implementation. One cannot always anticipate every eventuality, but leaders must be prepared to work on each as they arise.

5. *Lack of Support:* Devoting much time and effort to developing common values, beliefs, and purposes for multicultural education is essential to successful implementation. Moving from conflict to consensus involves building connections with others. Evans (1996) and Fullan (1993) found that a "critical mass" of the school's communities must support the innovation. There is no magical number to determine when enough people support a change before moving forward. Critical mass does not mean a majority or a certain percentage. Teacher leaders are invaluable in determining when this critical mass is apparent. This can be done through formal and informal conversations, open meetings with all staff, or individually with influential persons. Do not expect to have everyone on board. Some may disagree but are willing to try it. Others may continue their resistance through noncompliance.

In addition to the suggestions made earlier, both Evans and Fullan believe that "pressure" and use of "power" by leaders are ways to create broad-based commitment. Although coercion may be necessary with some, this is not to imply that this behavior by leaders is negative. Pressure can be applied by using one's influence within the school. A respected teacher leader's commitment to multicultural education is a form of such pressure. Allowing nonsupporters opportunities to voice their concerns provides needed incentive for some. Again, it is important first to determine why they do not support the innovation and then attempt to speak to their concerns before applying any sort of influence. It is inherently more precarious when the formal leadership applies pressure than when a teacher leader uses influence with a peer. Remember, lack of commitment may be due to confusion, absence of skills, or clarity of meaning. As professionals, teachers must be involved throughout the process of change, and teacher leaders must be knowledgeable in how the innovation may affect their fellow teachers.

Teacher Leadership Skills and Behaviors

Teaching is a passionate vocation, emotional, hard labor. Passions should never be ignored or dismissed, as is most often the case. In other words, all the best techniques in the world, all the best planned standards, all the resources that anyone could ever want, will mean nothing unless we address and help sustain the emotional needs of our students and teachers.—ELEMENTARY TEACHER, OAKLAND, CA

How does one become a teacher leader? Are leaders born or made? I believe every teacher has the capacity to become a leader. Every teacher is a leader in her or his classroom and exercises some degree of influence with colleagues. I make these statements in the connection with my definition of leadership. *Leadership* is a set of processes that enable the participants to construct individual meanings about the issues and use those understandings to develop a sense of common purpose. These processes engage all citizens of the school's communities (López, 1996). This definition does not refer to a person but rather to movements put into place through leadership.

Successful teacher leadership that influences schoolwide action requires preparation. Few preservice programs devote much, if any, time to leadership skills and behaviors. Administrator preparation programs, by their very nature, focus on these areas. But it is not necessary, nor is it advisable, that teacher leaders become administrators to provide leadership. Since administrators are separated from actual classroom instruction and constant student interactions, I do not suggest that teacher leaders have to assume administrative positions or roles to lead school change. They can be more credible and supportive of their colleagues by remaining in the classrooms. Certain behaviors can influence group discussion and eventual decisions (see **Figure 12.1**). The use of these skills effectively requires knowledge and understanding of these behaviors.

Summary

A school has many leaders. Formal leadership of administrators alone is insufficient to create successful schools for all students. Active, bold, socially responsible leadership is everyone's job in the schools. As I attempted to point out in this chapter, leadership requires new knowledge, skills, and preparation. Teachers, with active support from administrators and parents, must be in the forefront of creating schools that not only actively respect diversity but that also demonstrate that the schools value the many diverse cultures of the students.

Creating schools that value diversity of thinking and empowerment in a multicultural society requires having many opportunities to discuss what that would look like. These will be difficult conversations but they must occur before we can effectively provide all students with the type of education we want for our own children. What will these schools look like? The answer lies within the communities of the schools with teachers leading the effort.

FIGURE 12.1   Leadership Behaviors that Influence Groups

Initiating	Facilitating	Inquiring
Beginning something by raising a question, opening a topic, or adding to the agenda.	Keeping the conversation moving by inviting others to participate, and by summarizing, synthesizing, and moving the agenda (e.g., "Let's take a couple more comments on this and move on").	Asking directly for information that seeks a definite response; proposing new ways in which to gather, discover, or generate new information or ideas; and bringing information to the group for review and discussion.
Catalyzing	**Participating**	**Challenging**
Connecting people or ideas together, building of group ideas (e.g., "I think your comment supports what José has been saying..." "I would like to add to Linda's idea by giving an example").	Being a full participant by engaging in the process—listening, contributing, initiating, facilitating, inquiring, catalyzing, and challenging.	Taking exception with the prevailing thought or "group think," posing questions that challenge old or current assumptions and behaviors.
Acting	**Listening**	
Proposing approaches or solutions that address the issues with which the group is struggling. Ideas presented must not be in the discussion phase but rather in the problem-solving point of the discussion.	Asking questions for clarification, showing physically that one is listening (e.g., eye contact, posture), reinforcing or expanding comments to show understanding.	

References

Evans, R. (1996). *The human side of school change.* San Francisco: Jossey-Bass.

Fullan, F. G. (1991). *The meaning of educational change.* New York: Teachers College Press.

Fullan, F. G. (1993). *Change forces: Probing the depths of educational reform.* Bristol, PA: Falmer Press.

Hargraves, A. (1997). Rethinking educational change: Going deeper and wider in the quest for success. In A. Hargraves (Ed.), *Rethinking educational change with heart and mind* (pp. 1–26). Alexandria, VA: Association for Supervision and Curriculum Development.

Joyce, B., & Showers, B. (1995). *Student achievement through staff development* (2nd ed.). New York: Longman.

Lambert, L., Collay, M., Dietz, M. E., Kent, K., & Richert, A. E. (1996). *Who will save our schools?* Thousand Oaks, CA: Corwin Press.

Lambert, L., Walker, D., Cooper, J. E., Lambert, M. D., Gardner, M. E., & Ford Slack, P. J. (1995). *The constructivist leader.* New York: Teachers College Press.

López, J. A. (1996). "Taking Stock of Richmond High School: A University/Public School Partnership." *Proceedings of the International Management Association.* Toronto: International Management Association.

Oakes, J., & Lipton, M. (1999). *Teaching to change the world.* New York: McGraw-Hill.

Rallis, S. (1989). Professional teachers and restructured schools: Leadership challenges. In B. Mitchell & L. Cunningham (Eds.), *Educational leadership and changing contexts of families, communities, and schools: Eighty-ninth yearbook of the National Society for the Study of Education* (pp. 184–209). Chicago: University of Chicago Press.

Epilogue

Self-Transformation through Critical Literacy, Reflections, and Actions

JACQUELYN VALERIE REZA

*Speaking becomes both a way to engage in
active self-transformation and a rite of
passage where one moves from being
object to being subject. Only as subjects can we
speak. As objects, we remain voiceless—our
being defined and interpreted by others.*
—B. HOOKS (1989)

Moving toward Transformation

A transformative approach to multicultural education implies being
critically reflective of oneself as the instructor, professor, teacher,
facilitator, and student. Transformative theory has been thought

about, written about, and advocated by feminist scholars as well as scholars concerned with ethnopedagogy. Advocates among them are mentioned in the writings throughout this book. To be committed to transformative education, one must be willing to be transformed. It means dealing with the "ism" of life through a critically reflective process that includes the affective, cognitive, behavioral, and spiritual domains of both the personal and public areas of one's life.

The Two Sides of Our Experience

Critical Theory

At its foundation, transformative education sets critical pedagogy as its cornerstone, meaning that the empowerment process of all concerned occurs through the transformation of reality and of self (Ada & Beutel, 1993; Freire, 1974, 1994). Critical dialogic, a tenet of critical pedagogy, becomes the practice that creates an environment and structure through which student and teacher alike can find and follow their own inner processes moving toward transformation.

Within this context, change is held in a delicate balance, because the teacher/facilitator becomes the student and must honor the voice and will of those with whom he or she is working. Freire (1990) amplifies this perspective of change by calling it "a respect for the soul of the culture." He feels that the respect does not prevent him from trying to change conditions that appear to go against the beauty of being human.

Engaging in critical dialogue involves intentionally assessing the meaning of human existence and reality with the specific intent of creating a more socially just world. The emergence of an emancipatory voice is the result.

Oppression and Internalized Oppression

By accepting the premise of critical theory, one must address oneself on an interpersonal level, not just as a professional teacher but what one brings to the classroom in terms of personal experiences.

Each one of us as a critical educator has found our own liberation from oppressive factors that affect our lives. Oppression comes in many forms and its presence is evident in our students. It evolves slowly, with students from all ethnicities being affected. The degree present is seen in their behavior, appearance, and/or lack of participation.

Oppression is defined as having three components: (1) it can be part of the national consciousness, (2) an imbalance of power exists, and (3) it is reinforced within institutions. Examples of oppressions include, but are not limited to, classism, racism, sexism, anti-Semitism, adultism (this is the systematic oppression of children by adults), ageism, "able bodiedism," heterosexism (homophobia), and sizism/lookism.

In a society based on oppression, everyone (at one time or another) becomes socialized into the *role of being oppressed* and at alternate times into the *role of being the oppressor.* In any form of oppression, the role of the oppressor is ascribed to the *nontargeted* group. The oppressed is the *targeted* group.

Jackins's (1982) reevaluation theory is one of many theories available that addresses the interpersonal, affective element that needs to occur for an uncolonized voice to emerge. This theory starts with the assumption that all human beings are born "good," with an enormous amount of intelligence, curiosity, zest for life, and a sense of pride in being sentient beings.

Internalized Oppression

Over time, any group targeted by oppression inevitably "internalizes" the mistreatment and the misinformation about itself and then "mis-believes" some of the misinformation. This "mis-believing" expresses itself in behavior and interactions between members of the target group, which repeat the content of their oppression. *Internalized oppression is always an involuntary reaction to the experience of oppression on the part of the target group.* To blame the target group in any way for having internalized the consequences of their oppression is itself an act of oppression (Roybal Rose, 1989).

Internalized oppression is then manifested by becoming fixated on historical survival patterns that may not be appropriate at that moment. This occurs because of patterns that cause one to tolerate and proliferate internalized classism, sexism, adultism, anti-Semitism, and the oppression of other oppressed groups. Interpersonally and in one's home, the oppressor continues to manifest dysfunctional families and individual relationships, often putting unreasonable demands on one's children. The need to feel-good-now is fostered in an oppressive society and can lead to drug and/or alcohol addiction as well as workaholism. At home and in the school environment, people mistrust their own thinking, narrow their concepts of culture, and then act out their stereotypes of cultural misinformation. They do not allow themselves to become engaged in long-range goal setting or transformative learning. They attack the efforts of others, create disunity, and attack the leadership of others when they have the courage to step forward (Lipsky, 1987).

The Culture of Power

Until recently, *power* was defined as hierarchical, with a limited amount available, thus implying that to attain power meant that someone else had to lose power or become disempowered. Centriarchical concepts of power assert that there is an infinite amount of power and the more one gives power away, the more power is created (Helgesen, 1990).

From traditional leadership, *literature power* is defined in five ways: as coercive power, reward and coercion power, expert power, legitimate power, and charismatic power. This discussion of power leaves out external forces of control that frame one's self-concept of personal power. It assumes that power is either given or taken away. These forms of power can be seen within the classroom and within communities every day.

From a transformative perspective, power can be taken and used to empower those students who have been systematically marginalized, moving them from margin to center. To create multicultural transformative classrooms, both the explicit and implicit rules of power must be addressed, and the more teachers make the implicit rules of power explicit, the more they empower those who have been disempowered (Delpit, 1988). According to Delpit, the five tenets of power are:

1. Issues of power are enacted in all environments: work, classrooms, community(ies), and home.
2. There are codes or rules for participating in power; that is, there is a "culture of power."
3. The rules of the culture of power are a reflection of the rules of the culture of those who have power.
4. If you are not already a participant in the culture of power, being told explicitly the rules of that culture makes acquiring power easier.
5. Those with power are frequently least aware of—or least willing to acknowledge—its existence. Those with less power are often most aware of its existence.

Reclaiming our voices and facilitating the process of our students' voices means addressing oppression both internally and externally, both publicly and privately. One must be willing to address the affective component as well as cognitive/intellectual and behavioral components of pedagogy within the classroom, on campuses, and within communities as well as within one's own life.

Reflection

Once the "colonized" mind can identify *what* has been internalized (myth, fact, or misinformation), the person identifies *how* he or she has internalized the oppression. This awareness leads to encouraging individuals and groups of people to seek out and direct their attention to "noticing" their strengths, intelligence, greatness, power, and successes. The transformative work is that of constantly seeking out features of present culture, of engaging in praxis about those features of culture that are not benign but are in reality oppressions and responses to oppression and that have kept the colonized trapped in a cycle of oppression-internalized oppression. Power is used to create this oppressive reality.

What We Can Do about It

In *Lives on the Boundary,* Rose (1989) uses the analogy of the lens of a camera. There is a standard lens through which people see the world and, in order to redefine their reality, people must be taught to "refocus" that lens or change it, thus redefining reality:

> *To truly educate in America, then, to reach the full sweep of our citizenry, we need to question received perception, shift continually from the standard lens. Encourage [ourselves] to sit close by as people use language and consider, as we listen to the orientations that limit our field of vision. (Rose, 1989)*

Critical theory puts forward the perceptions of a group's reality; it then asks the group to reflect on *its* knowledge. Critical pedagogy then takes what the *group* determines is important and what contributes to its own liberation and frames the knowledge in a way that leads to social change. Critical pedagogy calls for political action that comes from the liberatory voice of the participants engaged in critical reflection and dialogue.

The commitment to being transformative is an active, ongoing process that involves diligent, critical reflection from the cognitive, affective, and behavioral domains. We need to think about what is happening. We need to be aware of how we feel, because feelings are an indication of beliefs, values, and morals. They let us know that "something's up." Once feelings and thoughts associated with a particular situation have been duly processed, then behavioral changes will occur with less stress. The changes will feel more natural because it is *in our nature* to change behavior in order to obtain a greater congruence of thought and feeling. We start by listening—not just any listening but one that will enhance the process of transformation. The "art of listening" (Jackins, 1981) without imposing one's own beliefs is to increase the hearing of the liberatory voice of those who have been oppressed.

The Liberatory Voice

Transformative multicultural education approaches have not yet been deeply explored, discussed, recognized, or realized in the literature. This book is about regaining an uncolonized voice in education from a transformative multicultural perspective, reflective of communities that have historically been excluded from our educational system. By reclaiming an ethnopedagogical voice vis-à-vis education, a more inclusive form of education evolves and validates those who have not found their kind, their selves, their experiences reflected in the academe. Multicultural classrooms are no longer a prospect of the future or something alien that we have to worry about. Our classrooms are varied and rainbow in nature, as our pedagogy should be. Critical literacy in a multicultural classroom deserves to be explored, discussed, dialogued about, voiced, and named in as many venues as possible.

Language is powerful and essential in developing one's voice, in defining one's cultural identity, and in naming the world for oneself. Gaining a liberated voice means "creating strategies that will enable colonized folks to decolonize their minds and actions, thereby promoting the insurrection of subjugated knowledge" (hooks, 1990).

Coming to a critical consciousness is painful and requires the colonized to question the existing paradigm creating a dissonance through which they can regain their emancipatory voice. "The colonized have become participants in the daily rituals of power... that reinforce and maintain our positions as the dominated" (hooks, 1990). The process of critical consciousness requires courage and the strength to struggle against the "truths" of the oppressor to know and honor one's own truth. Doing the hard work of transformation requires dedication, the willingness to accept that we will make mistakes, and constant reflection. We must indeed trust the process and remember always that it is a process.

References

Ada, A. F., & Beutel, C. M. (1993). *Participatory research as a dialogue for social action.* Unpublished manuscript, University of San Francisco.

Delpit, L. D. (1988). The silenced dialogue: Power and pedagogy in educating other people's children. *Harvard Educational Review 58* (3).

Freire, P. (1974/1990). *Pedagogy of the oppressed* (Myra Bergman Ramos, Trans.). New York: Seabury Press.

Freire, P. (1994). *Pedagogy of hope: Reliving pedagogy of the oppressed* (R. Barr, Trans.). New York: Continuum.

Glaserfeld, V. E. (1989, July). Cognition, construction of knowledge, and teaching. *Synthese 80,* pp. 121–140.

Helgesen, S. (1990). *The female advantage: Women's ways of leadership.* New York: Doubleday Currency.

hooks, b. (1989). *Talking back.* Boston: South End Press.

hooks, b. (1990). *Yearning: Race, gender, and cultural politics.* Boston: South End Press.

Horton, M., & Freire, P. (1990). *We make the road by walking.* Philadelphia: Temple University Press.

Jackins, H. (1981). *The art of listening.* Seattle: Rational Island Publishers.

Jackins, H. (1982). *The human side of human beings: The theory of re-evaluation counseling.* Seattle: Rational Island Publishers.

Jue, J. (1993). *Chinese American women's development of voice and cultural identity: A participatory research study via feminist oral history.* Unpublished doctoral dissertation, University of San Francisco.

Lipsky, S. (1987) *Internalized racism.* Seattle: Reevaluation Counseling Foundation.

Reinharz, S. (1998). *The concept of voice.* Paper presented at a conference on Human Diversity, Department of Psychology, University of Maryland.

Rose, M. (1989). *Lives on the boundary.* New York: Penguin.

Roybal Rose, L. (1989). *Cross cultural communication workshops.* Cross Cultural Communication, 256 Towhee Dr., Santa Cruz, CA 95060.

Sherover-Marcuse, R. (1989). *Liberation theory: Part I. Axioms and working assumptions about the perpetuation of social oppression.* Unlearning Racism Workshops, 6501 Dana, Oakland, CA 94609.

Weissglass, J. (1990). Constructivist listening for empowerment and change. *The Educational Forum 54* (4), 351–370.

Index